IN 1933 millions of people in the western world had no jobs and little food. This was the height of the economic blizzard which tore across the world in 1929 and only abated in the mid-1930s. Its catalyst, though not its cause, was the dramatic Wall Street crash. The financial crisis which followed reacted on weak national economies to bring about the Great Depression.

The results were appalling in terms of human misery, as the author shows. In the shadow of mass unemployment living conditions deteriorated, and became a fertile breeding ground for extremist politics, notably Communism and Fascism. Indeed, politics for the next decade were conditioned by the slump. Even in states where extremists were denied political power, as in Britain and France, grave political crises ensued. The author illustrates how the world responded to crisis in the dictatorships of Germany and Italy and in the democracies of France, Britain and the United States, and finds a surprising similarity between remedies such as Mussolini's Corporate State and Roosevelt's New Deal.

Yet government action was hamstrung by orthodox faith in the gold standard and in balanced budgets. Men were bewildered that, in the affluent twentieth century, the world could so defy man's control. The period from the Wall Street crash to the coming of the Second World War brought a slow evolution of new economic ideas, pioneered by John Maynard Keynes, to restore full employment and to ensure that the world should never again be so afflicted.

This addition to the WAYLAND DOCUMENTARY HISTORY SERIES draws on speeches, state papers, private papers and diaries, political manifestoes, newspapers, journals, novels and poetry to recreate the men, events and ideas of these turbulent years.

The Great Depression

Marion Yass

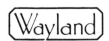

Cover: Jarrow marchers passing through the village of Lavendon in Bedfordshire on their way to London (26.10.36)
Frontispiece: British unemployed workers staging a hunger march during the Great Depression

First published in 1973 by
Wayland (Publishers) Ltd
61 Western Road, Hove
East Sussex BN3 1JD

© Copyright 1973 Wayland (Publishers) Ltd

Second impression 1988

ISBN 1 85210 595 X

Printed and bound at
The Bath Press, Avon, England

Contents

The Illustrations

1 The Roaring Twenties

THE PHRASE "the Roaring Twenties" conjures up a picture of *America*
enormous and excited prosperity in the United States. Americans
in power during those years shared this view. During his 1928
Presidential campaign, Herbert Hoover claimed that "we in
America today are nearer to the final triumph over poverty than
ever before in the history of any land. The poorhouse is vanishing
from among us (1)." Later the same year, the outgoing President,
Calvin Coolidge, told Congress in his last address that "no
Congress of the United States ever assembled . . . has met with a
more pleasing prospect than that which appears at the present
time. In the domestic field there is tranquillity and contentment
[and] the highest record of years of prosperity (2)."

This was America's carnival age. It was an age when millions of
people went to watch the movies of Rudolf Valentino; when
sports like football, baseball, basketball and boxing drew million-
dollar gates at the new enormously lavish city stadiums that had
been constructed.

Hoover attributed this prosperity to the American pioneering *Pioneering*
spirit: "By our energies in invention and enterprise we had raised *spirit*
our *per capita* productivity to levels never hitherto known in the
world. Various economic studies showed that in the twenties our
productivity per person increased by over thirty per cent (3)."
Two of the items Hoover had in mind, both key factors in the
new prosperity, were mass production and hire purchase. Mass
production methods were a startling revelation to Oswald Mosley
when he first visited the United States in 1926. He recalls in his
autobiography that "the industrial tour was one of the most

Mass production of automobiles: a New York traffic jam in the 1920s interesting experiences of my life . . . I watched men working at the conveyor belt in the Ford factory. Each performed some simple operation on the vehicle in the making as it reached him on the conveyor . . . it was simplicity itself . . . This was a new world of industry . . . The Ford factory produced the cheapest article and paid the highest wage in the world; in terms of money value, nothing on earth could compare with that original Tin Lizzie. Mass production for a large and assured home market is the industrial key (4)."

Ford   In 1927 one writer noted how far Ford operations had grown by the time the new Model A was launched: "Starting on Monday the Ford Company began printing a series of five daily full page advertisements in 2,000 papers throughout the country. Samples of the new car will be shown on Friday in the principal cities (5)."

The Ford motor car became the symbol of the decade; and "a car in every garage and a chicken in every pot" the Republican slogan in the 1928 election campaign. As mass production had drastically cut costs, and as the instalment or hire purchase system grew, more and more people were able to buy more and more products. The American correspondent of *The Economist* devoted a whole column to explaining the novel instalment system: "The automobile manufacturers encouraged it through a desire to increase sales and reduce the unit costs of production. Automobiles account for $1,500 millions of the instalment debt at the present time. Household furniture is the second commodity in importance. It is estimated that 80 per cent of all gramophones are sold on instalments, 75 per cent of washing machines, 65 per cent of vacuum cleaners, 25 per cent of all jewellery and the greater part of all pianos, sewing machines, wireless apparatus and electric refrigerators (6)."

An advertisement for *True Story Magazine*'s feature, "Story of Personal Credit," appeared in the *New York Herald Tribune*, praising the results of the system: "Any of you who are willing to get up early enough can look out of your own windows and see a trail of thousands of workmen's automobiles scooting down the boulevards to their factory or new building destination. Even ten years ago this great mass of labour had to live just around the corner in a hovel next to the factory or hang on street cars at six o'clock in the morning in order to reach the building operation (7)."

The workers owned cars; the middle classes owned washing machines and, from 1925, turned to real estate investment, especially in Florida. A contemporary, Frederick Lewis Allen, wrote that Miami "had become one frenzied real estate exchange. There were said to be 2,000 real estate offices and 25,000 agents marketing house lots or acreage . . . Motor buses roared down Flagler Street carrying 'prospects' on free trips to watch dredgers and steam shovels converting the outlying mangrove swamps . . . into gorgeous Venetian cities for the American home makers and pleasure seekers of the future (8)." Oswald Mosley saw plots of land "being bought and sold over and over again in frantic speculation, and prices were astronomical. Rocks out in the sea were being acquired for some future mythical construction (9)." It was the coming of the motor car and, in Allen's words, "the abounding confidence engendered by Coolidge prosperity, which persuaded the four thousand dollar a year salesman that, in some magical way, he too might tomorrow be able to buy a fine house and all the good things of the earth (10)." *Real estate*

"In 1928 there were thirty-one bank failures in Florida, in 1929 there were fifty-seven," wrote Allen (11). The land boom had collapsed. O. G. Villard passed along the Miami road and wrote in his newspaper *The Nation* that "dead subdivisions line the highway, their pompous names half obliterated on crumbling stucco gates . . . Whole sections are composed of unoccupied houses past which one speeds as if traversing a city in the grip of death (12)." But the failure was blamed on hurricanes which had torn through the city. The mood of get-rich-quick optimism survived and gained strength from Coolidge's December, 1928, speech; Coolidge told Congress: "Regard the present with satisfaction and anticipate the future with optimism (13)." *Bank failures*

This is exactly what the average American citizen did. According to Frederick Allen, he "saw a magical order built on the new science and the new prosperity: roads swarming with millions upon millions of automobiles, airplanes darkening the skies . . . vast cities rising [and] smartly dressed men and women spending, spending (14)."

President Calvin Coolidge addressing Congress

Stock Market Much of this spending took place on the Stock Market; after all, why should the boom end? As one financial editor wrote, "The American citizen has had it drummed into his head that there never was in the world before anything like present-day America, 'The Land of Unlimited Possibilities.' Therefore he has felt that no arguments drawn from previous experience applied to America. Booms have always hitherto been followed by slumps but then that was either outside America or else a long time ago. Post-war America is the country which never gets tired, never loses nerve and courage (15)."

The Economist agreed that wild optimism was the basis of growing speculation: "The American investor got the idea so firmly into his head that the future of his country was marvellously bright and rising industrial profits absolutely certain that industrial shares seemed to him good things to buy even at a price which provided a tiny present income (16)." So long as the market kept rising he could always sell at a profit tomorrow. Another newspaper pointed out, when it was all over, that speculation rested on "the belief, widely acted upon if not consciously realized, that it was possible to buy a security for a certain sum of money, to sell it again later for a higher price and to continue the process indefinitely (17)." Share prices were now soaring way beyond the real value of the companies they represented.

Even those with small savings turned to the Stock Market. *Ticker tapes* "The speculative public includes artisans, lift boys, clerks and waitresses as well as businessmen and others of more substantial means," the *Evening Standard* told its London readers (18). Frederick Allen said that in 1927 "one did not have to listen long to an after-dinner conversation, whether in New York or San Francisco or the lowliest village of the plain, to realize that all sorts of people to whom the stock ticker had been a hitherto alien mystery were carrying a hundred shares of Studebaker or Houston Oil [and] whipping the early editions of afternoon papers to catch the 1.30 quotations from Wall Street (19)." The *Evening Standard* pointed out that "in America the dissemination of Stock Exchange news and prices by tape machines and other devices and the furnishing of lounges for clients in city offices had tended to make speculation easy (20)."

If it was easy for the small man to make money, it was easier still for the rich industrialist or film magnate. Profits from mass production released more capital for investment in the Stock Market. Fortunes were doubled and trebled. A table of incomes in the United States in 1926 showed "the extreme opulence of the wealthier classes of Americans. Roughly speaking there are well over five or six times as many persons in the super tax class in the United States as in Great Britain, whereas the American population is less than three times as large as the British population (21)."

The novelist, Scott Fitzgerald, who was writing his superb novels *Charleston* at this time drew a brilliant picture of the luxurious life led by *age* the ultra rich. In 1926 he wrote in *The Great Gatsby*: "There was music from my neighbour's house through the summer nights. In his blue gardens men and girls came and went like moths

15

among the whisperings and the champagne and the stars . . . On buffet tables, furnished with glistening hors-d'oeuvres spiced baked hams crowded against salads of harlequin designs and pastry pigs and turkeys bewitched to a dark gold (22)."

The reality was as wild and opulent as the fiction, as Derek Patmore, an English visitor to New York soon found: "Charleston! Charleston! . . . Thin spindly legs encased in silk stockings . . . stamped out frenzied rhythms each night on the polished floors of the night clubs and the mirrored walls echoed to the tinkle of ice dropped into innumerable highballs. The people of New York . . . were indulging in an orgy of parties. The search for pleasure was frantic and money was no longer counted (23)."

The guests at Gatsby's parties and the dancers at the clubs visited by Patmore all sang the popular tune:

> In the morning,
> In the evening,
>   Ain't we got fun!
> One thing's sure and nothing's surer,
> The rich get richer, and the poor get—children.

Disparity of wealth
Here was one of the crucial flaws in the American economy: the unequal distribution of wealth. The rich themselves felt this discrepancy. Cornelius Vanderbilt Jnr., the heir of the great press tycoon, wrote in his autobiography that "before the nationwide depression and the New Deal which would challenge and change many American views, great wealth in itself was supposed to set one apart. It was felt by many people, and certainly by my family . . . that we were not 'ordinary people' (24)." This inequality was a dangerous time-fuse; for businessmen's profits depended upon the spending power of the ordinary American.

Describing the opulence and numbers of the wealthy, *The Economist* declared that "alongside this great wealth there exists in America very great poverty also (25)." Despite Hoover's optimism the poorhouse had not vanished after all. Oswald Mosley saw for himself the slums of New York and the "still prevailing areas of poverty and degradation," as well as Florida and the factories. When Robert and Helen Lynd carried out their study of Middletown as a typical small American city in 1929 they heard such comments as: "We have been buying no fresh

Buyers in a New York stockbroker's office jubilant at the upward movement of share prices (1929)

milk this year," and from a family of five, "Our living expenses are never more than five dollars a week (26)."

Poverty was worse in country districts than in the towns. In October, 1927, one newspaper summarized the Report on Economic Conditions in the U.S.A., drawn up by the Development of Overseas Trade: "There is still a wide margin between agricultural and general industrial prices, and the position of some sections of the farming community, which has been a weak link in the chain of general prosperity, continues to be unsettled and uncertain (27)."

In his Congressional address of April, 1929, President Hoover explained some of the farmers' difficulties: "Disorderly and wasteful methods of marketing have developed. The growing specialization in the industry [has] been increasing the proportion of products that now leave the farm, and prices have been unduly depressed (28)." A financial editor observed that "the people of America tend to fall into two classes, traders and farmers ... Throughout the long stock boom [there] have been millions of people expecting some day to see the money changers driven out of the American temple (29)."

17

Wall Street speculators watching the ticker tape in early 1929

The discrepancies between the fantastic wealth and struggling poverty, and between town and country, belied Calvin Coolidge's claim early in 1929 that things were "absolutely sound." So did the character of some of the loans backed by speculators. Since the Great War (1914–18) America had become Europe's creditor. Every European nation owed her war debts. In order to pay these, and to strengthen their war-damaged economies, foreign governments floated loans subscribed by private American speculators. "By 1922," wrote Hoover, "a boom began in foreign loans with the offer by foreign countries of extravagant interest to private lenders from 5 per cent to 8 per cent (30)." The economist, John Maynard Keynes, told Chicago students at a seminar that "rates of interest were high indeed. A comparatively small country like the republic of Colombia . . . found itself able to borrow something like the $200 millions in New York within a brief space of time (31)." Such enormous loans were often insecure. Hoover stressed at the 1927 Pan American conference "that no nation as a government should borrow and no government lend . . . unless this money is to be devoted to productive enterprise. Out of the wealth created from enterprise itself must come the ability to repay (32)."

War debts

But many were not repaid. As early as 1922 (and many more such loans were floated in the next seven years) Hoover could write that "securities in foreign currencies have been sold to the American investor which have resulted in a national loss of probably upwards of five hundred millions of dollars in the last three years (33)."

Speculation in risky foreign loans, and in over-priced shares, meant that fortunes were quickly won and lost. Mosley met "the end product of American success, the fabulous millionaires; men like Josh Cosden who was reputed to have started punching tickets on a tram and to have won, lost and won again three big fortunes before he was forty (34)."

Money was also lost through bank failures. "The public had become callous to bank failures," wrote Hoover, "because we had over 4,000 such failures in the eight good years before the depression. A weak banking system [was] another of our domestic ills . . . Dangers were present in our inexpressibly feeble and badly

Banking

President Calvin Coolidge

organized deposit banking, credit and security promotion structure, enhanced by lack of scruples among some leaders. There were too many banks, there simply were not enough capable bankers to go around among 25,000 banks . . . More than 3,500 had less than $100,000 capital and of these some 1,500 had less than $25,000 capital. A safe banking life . . . simply could not be led on such capital (35)."

This weak banking structure, the unsound speculation and the unequal distribution of wealth were the major flaws in the American economy. They were soon to end the unprecedented riches and "unbounding optimism" of the Roaring Twenties.

2 Black Thursday on Wall Street

Signs of danger

BY 1929 a few discerning people began to sense the dangers of the situation. The Governor of New York State, Franklin D. Roosevelt, criticized "the fever of speculation (36)." Writing in his autobiography about the public mood late that summer, Cornelius Vanderbilt Jnr. said that "in this country some people still coasted on a wave of prosperity which, we were told by those in power, would never end. I had another idea. I had talked to Professor Irving Fisher up at Yale and he had told me a crash was coming. I tried to convey the information to my father, who said Yale's famous economist was a crazy old coot and he didn't care to hear what he had to say (37)."

But the wary were in a small minority. Like Vanderbilt Snr., and "those in power," most people preferred to shut their eyes to the dangers. On 22nd October, only two days before the great Wall Street crash, the Chairman of the National City Bank, Charles E. Mitchell, knew of "nothing fundamentally wrong with the Stock Market or with the underlying business and credit structure (38)." Whether sincere or expedient, statements like Mitchell's had their effect on the speculating public.

Speculation

Frederick Lewis Allen described how, for many people, the Stock Exchange became a frantic way of life: "How many Americans actually held stock on margin during the fabulous summer of 1929 there seems to be no way of computing; but it is probably safe to put the figure at more than a million . . . The rich man's chauffeur drove with his ears laid back to catch the news of an impending move in Bethlehem Steel; he held fifty shares himself . . . The window-cleaner at the broker's office paused to watch the ticker, for he was thinking of putting his laboriously accumulated savings into a few shares of Simmons. A broker's valet [made] nearly a quarter of a million in the market; a trained nurse . . . cleaned up thirty thousand following the tips given her by grateful patients.

"An ex-actress in New York fitted up her Park Avenue apartment as an office and surrounded herself with charts, graphs, and financial reports, playing the market by telephone on an increasing scale and with increasing abandon. Thousands speculated, and won too, without the slightest knowledge of the nature of the company upon whose fortunes they were relying. Grocers, motormen, plumbers, seamstresses and speakeasy waiters were in the market . . . The Big Bull Market had become a national mania (39)."

Looking back with the wisdom of a month's hindsight, the London press found "growing recognition of the fact that the background for the decline was set by the excessive capital flotations of the summer and autumn [and] by the recession in industry that began in July (40)." The speculators were too busy with the ticker tapes to notice any cracks in the plaster. But the cracks were there. Industrial production reached a peak in June, but dropped in July. In 1929 investment in home construction fell more than a billion dollars below the 1928 figure.

Post-war problems

President Hoover explained this recession partly by the fact that industry had filled the production gap left by the 1914–18 war: "During the war, building construction, industrial equipment and capital goods generally had to be suspended to make way for war supplies . . . Coming out of the war we had two capital goods economies: one carrying on the immediate need of a growing population and industry, and the other busily catching up with the war suspensions. We needed, say, 400,000 new dwellings annually for population growth and for the replacement of worn out buildings. We were compelled to increase construction to about 800,000 houses to catch up with losses during the war and to meet the current demand. This applied in many directions, [to] power, railways, highways and many capital goods. But when we had caught up with the lag, that whole section of our economy slumped (41)."

Left The optimistic President Herbert Hoover; *right* New Yorkers throng
Wall Street during the Great Crash of 1929

The July recession destroyed the wild speculation within twelve weeks. Shares suddenly plummetted as its effect shook the Stock Market. For the first time doubt was cast upon the road to easy riches. The panic of the crash was as contagious as the wild optimism of the boom. A newspaperman wrote that "nothing happened to cause the collapse, except the pricking of the bubble (42)." Once there was "a revulsion of feeling (43)" this collapse could not be halted.

Gerald Heard remembered this aspect of the crash: "Material wealth had not been destroyed. All the misery and ruin was due, not to an economic fact, but to a psychological state of mind. Credit had been shaken, and credit, it was proved, though not a material fact, can nevertheless give such seismic shocks to the material prosperity of millions that they may be reduced to begging their bread (44)."

The crash came on Thursday, 24th October, aptly christened
Black Thursday. The market fell and there was wild selling. "The
Stock Market," declared the *New York Herald Tribune*, "was
shaken to its foundations [by] the severest break in the history of
Wall Street. The immediate cause of the debacle, which was
entirely unexpected, was the forced liquidation of large brokerage
accounts (45)."

The *Evening Standard* explained to its curious London readers
that "the usual method of speculation consists of operating on
margin. When a purchase of stock is made a fixed margin in price
has to be put up by the buyer. If the price rises he can sell and take
a profit, but if it falls he must put up more cash to maintain a
margin or have his stock sold at a loss. On a rapidly falling market
thousands of accounts may be uncovered simultaneously and
shares may be thrown on the market regardless of price. That is
what has been happening during the last few days (46)."

Frederick Lewis Allen painted a dramatic picture of Black
Thursday: "On that momentous day stocks opened moderately
steady in price, but in enormous volume. Kennecott appeared on
the tape in a block of 20,000 shares, General Motors in another
of the same amount. Almost at once the ticker tape began to lag
behind the trading on the floor. The pressure of selling orders was
disconcertingly heavy. Prices were going down . . . Presently they
were going down with some rapidity . . . Before the first hour of
trading was over, it was already apparent that they were going
down with an altogether unprecedented and amazing violence.

"In brokers' offices all over the country, tape-watchers looked
at one another in astonishment and perplexity. Where on earth
was this torrent of selling orders coming from? As the price
structure crumbled there was a sudden stampede to get out from
under. By eleven o'clock traders on the floor of the Stock Exchange
were in a wild scramble to 'sell at the market.' Long before the
flagging ticker could tell what was happening, word had gone out
by telephone and telegraph that the bottom was dropping out of
things, and the selling orders redoubled in volume.

"Down, down, down . . . Where were the bargain hunters who
were supposed to come to the rescue at a time like this? Where
were the investment trusts, which were expected to provide a

cushion for the market by making new purchases at low prices? Where were the powerful bankers who were supposed to be able at any moment to support prices? There seemed to be no support whatever. Down, down, down. The roar of voices which rose from the floor of the Exchange had become a roar of panic (47)."

Next day's London press carried an account of the panic under banner headlines "£1,000,000,000 crash on New York Stock Exchange. Wild selling in record turnover of 13,000,000 Shares. The heavy break on the New York Stock Exchange reached catastrophic proportions yesterday with a crash described as the worst in the history of the Exchange. The floor of the Exchange was a scene of the wildest excitement. Pandemonium reigned all day. The shouts of the frenzied brokers, fighting on the floor of the Exchange to sell their stocks at the best available prices could be heard in the street (48)."

Tourists flocked to listen to the noise and watch the panic-stricken dealers. "Wall Street was crowded with sightseers, and charabanc touring companies have diverted their big vehicles from other routes to take the curious to the scene (49)."

President Hoover tried to reassure the American public. He was supported by the *New York Herald Tribune* on 26th October: "The Stock Market held up like a stone wall yesterday . . . Reassurances that the country and business remain unshaken came yesterday from President Hoover . . . The Press said that there was nothing in the country's fundamental business conditions to cause uneasiness (50)." But three days later the *Herald Tribune* had to report that, "struck by renewed scare selling and forced liquidation, the Stock Market yesterday capped last Thursday's climax by scoring the greatest decline on record and completing the erasure of approximately all gains made this year (51)." Describing events on that same day, *The Economist* in London observed that "six years ago a daily turnover of one million shares on Wall Street was considered a high total; but on Tuesday over sixteen million shares changed hands, and on Wednesday nearly eleven millions (52)."

The excitement and activity was exhausting. "The decision of the authorities to close the Stock Exchange completely till noon on Thursday and for the whole of Friday and Saturday was

Hoover's reassurance

welcomed as affording an opportunity of recovery for overworked personnel and shattered nerves (53)." Other journalists noted the same tension: "Stock Exchange houses had worked all day on Sunday in straightening out accounts after the hectic three days, and overwrought and bleary eyed men and women of the clerical force face the prospect of working again all night tonight ... Doctors report a sudden increase in the number of their patients. The aftermath of a bad break in the market expresses itself in nervous diseases (54)."

Panic   The strain was too much for some. The same day the *Evening Standard* reported under large headlines that "during the excitement today Mr. J. J. Bell died in the New York Market. Trading was suspended for two minutes (55)." But selling began immediately afterwards.

The panic was said to have caused the suicides of many ruined men. Frederick Allen noted that "incredible rumours had spread wildly during the early afternoon" of Black Thursday, together with stories that "troops were guarding the New York Stock Exchange against an angry mob (56)." Two men who held a joint account were said to have jumped hand in hand from a high window of the Ritz Hotel. Indeed, there was some basis for these stories. J. J. Riordan, President of the County Trust Company, "took a pistol from his bank and went home to shoot himself in comfort (57)."

Later studies have shown such tales to be wildly exaggerated. This correspondent thought so, too: "Wall Street has been interested and amused at the descriptions of the recent break that have appeared in certain sections of your stunt press. Stories of streets clogged with the bodies of suicides [reveal] modern journalism at its worst. The confusion during the big break was very great and the wiping out of paper profits was tremendous. The losses suffered by the speculative public are very considerable [but] in New York City there were only two or three suicides that appear to have been prompted by the debacle in stocks (58)."

Small savers   There was misery enough without suicides. "Millions of wage
ruined   earners," read one report just after Black Thursday, "or poorly paid professional workers, had invested all or a large part of their

accumulated funds, in carrying stocks on margin; and these are

the people who were wiped out [in] yesterday's decline (59)."
Frederick Allen was, typically, more graphic: "The Big Bull
Market was dead. Billions of dollars' worth of profits [had] dis-
appeared. The grocer, the window-cleaner, and the seamstress had
lost their capital. In every town there were families which had
suddenly dropped from showy affluence into debt. Investors who
had dreamed of retiring to live on their fortunes now found themselves back once more at the very beginning of the long road to
riches. The post-war decade had come to its close. An era had
ended (60)."

Many Americans still refused to acknowledge that the decade of
prosperity was dead. After the crash, William Green of the
American Federation of Labour declared that "in a few months we
will be back to normal;" Stuart Chase, the economist, believed
that "the Stock Market collapse will not affect our general prosperity (61)," and Secretary of the Treasury Mellon assured everyone that 1930 would be "a normal year."

Obstinate optimism among the nation's leaders, if not among
the newly destitute, persisted into the Spring of 1930. President
Hoover felt "convinced we have now passed the worst, and with
continued unity of effort we shall rapidly recover (62)." Mary
Agnes Hamilton, a visitor to New York, commented that although
"in 1930 people were, of course, dazed and reeling under the
shock of the Wall Street and Stock Market collapse [few] could
really believe in it. Nearly everybody then said that it was temporary ... Prosperity, in fact, as a line in a witty Broadway
comedy put it with angry irony, was 'Hoovering' round the
corner (63)."

Obstinate optimism

President Hoover himself later justified his optimism during the
days of the crash, and even in 1930: "The press insistently urged
that I make a statement. Obviously, as President I had no business
to make things worse in the middle of a crash. Loath to speak
of the Stock Market, I offered as encouragement a short statement
on our progress in the productive system and the long-view
strength of the country (64)."

But Hoover was not only blamed later for his unsound optimism and his failure to remedy the effects of the crash; he was
accused of responsibility for that crash. In the 1932 election

Hoover's guilt

campaign, Roosevelt's first indictment of his opponent was that his government had "encouraged speculation through its false economic policies." But Hoover did not become President until March, 1929; clearly, the seeds of the crash were sown long before then.

On the other hand, Hoover was Secretary of Commerce under Coolidge and in a position to exert influence. He was not blind to the growing dangers of the 1920s. In his *Memoirs* he wrote: "During 1925 I began to be alarmed over the growing tide of speculation and gave warnings as to the dangers of this mood. In a press statement on New Years Day, 1926, I said: 'There are some phases of the situation which require caution . . . real estate and stock speculation and its possible extension into commodities with inevitable inflation; the over extension of instalment buying; the continued instability of certain foreign countries . . .' During 1926 I continued to issue warnings that the reckless speculation could undermine our prosperity (65)."

Hoover sounded many warnings but took very little action. For this he blamed his colleagues. He complained in the Spring of 1927, that when he wanted to stop the Federal Reserve Board making loans to European bankers, "Mr. Coolidge [insisted] that he could not interfere. The Secretary of the Treasury, Mr. Mellon, also declined and seemed to think my anxiety was alarmist and my interference unwarranted (66)." But when Hoover became President in his turn he did not dismiss Mellon from office. Neither was he readier than Coolidge or Mellon to step in to regulate the banks or the Stock Market. Hoover merely talked to the bankers who "scoffed at the idea that the market was not sound," and was equally loath to press the matter with the Stock Exchange itself. He made an effort "to send for the President of the New York Stock Exchange and urge that the Exchange itself curb the manipulation of stocks. I informed him that I had no desire to stretch the powers of the Federal Government by legislation to regulate the Stock Exchange (67)."

Hindsight   It is possible that, by government intervention, Hoover might have mitigated both speculation and recession. As it was he allowed boom, crash and slump to take their terrible course. Hoover himself admitted that "we could have done better—in retrospect (68)."

28

3 Chains of Gold

PRESIDENT Herbert Hoover underestimated the effects of the Wall Street crash. He disowned any guilt for the horrors of the Great Depression which followed: "The depth of our recession during the first seventeen months did not constitute a major depression and our internal strength enabled us to begin a strong convalescence. Had no external influences struck us it is certain that we should have passed out of the slump shortly . . . We could not but be affected by the degenerative forces moving elsewhere in the world." Hoover claimed that "the great centre of the storm was Europe. That storm moved slowly until the Spring of 1931 when it burst into a financial hurricane. At that moment the enormous war destruction, the economic consequences of the Treaty of Versailles, revolutions, unbalanced budgets, hugely increased armaments [finally] broke through all efforts to fend off their explosive forces (69)."

Hoover disclaims

But the effects of the 1914–18 war cannot in themselves be blamed for the Great Depression. As John Maynard Keynes told his Chicago students, by 1925 "the perturbations which had, perhaps inevitably, ensued on the war and the treaty of peace and the readjustments of economic relations between different countries, seemed to have about run their course. Confidence was more or less restored (70)." President Hoover failed to link the Depression with the disruption of the world monetary system upon which all western economies depended. The legacy of the war certainly helped this disruption, but the final and resounding blow was struck by the Wall Street crash.

A British bank in 1925, the year Britain returned to the Gold Standard

Professor Lionel Robbins described the prevailing monetary system. "For forty years before the war," he wrote, "the financial systems of the leading countries of the world had been linked together by the international gold standard. For a century the gold standard had been virtually effective. Trade between different national areas took place on the basis of rates of exchange which fluctuated between very narrow limits (71)." Gold had its advantages, as Keynes rather cynically pointed out: "As all of us know, gold has much to recommend it as a standard of value. It is portable, durable, uniform in quality, readily divisible . . . it has all those virtues which have sufficed to make [it] the basis of our monetary system (72)." Each currency had a fixed value in relation to gold, and therefore to each other. During the war every country except the United States abandoned this basis for their currencies and went off the gold standard. There followed a period of financial chaos. Professor Robbins echoed Keynes in thinking that, "by the middle of the twenties, the intense disorder had come to an end. One by one budgets were balanced and disordered currencies were restored to some kind of stability. In the Spring of

30

1925 Great Britain returned to the gold standard (73)."

Winston Churchill, then Chancellor of the Exchequer, announced this decision to the British House of Commons. He reminded Members that the Gold and Silver Act of 1920 had continued Britain's wartime departure from the gold standard. "We have decided to allow it to lapse," he said. "A return to an effective gold standard has long been the settled and declared policy of this country. Every expert conference since the war . . . every expert committee in this country has urged the principle of a return to the gold standard. It has always been taken as a matter of course that we should return to it (74)." *Britain returns to gold (1925)*

"Mr. Churchill has done what was expected," wrote Keynes in the *New Republic*. A return to the gold standard meant no more than having a fixed exchange rate. The more important question was what that rate should be. Keynes warned that by returning to the pre-war rate, Churchill had over-valued the pound: "We shall do well to remember that there is no means in the long run of maintaining the parity except by so managing our credit as to establish a gold price-level here not higher than the gold price-levels of other countries . . . If we must have a gold standard, we had better play the gold standard game according to the recognized rules (75)."

The over-valuation of the pound had a catastrophic effect on British exports. Overseas buyers found British raw materials and manufactured goods too costly. As Keynes put it, "The prices of British exports in the international market are too high . . . We are still asking in sterling just as much for our exports as when sterling was worth 12 per cent less in exchange value . . . This alteration in the external value of sterling money has been the deliberate act of the British government and the present troubles of our export industries are the inevitable and predictable consequence of it (76)." Imports were correspondingly cheaper for the British to buy. Similarly, British as well as foreign investors preferred to send their gold to countries where interest rates were higher and where they need not fear devaluation. *Sterling over-valued*

There was another deep reason why too much money flowed in one direction, upsetting the world monetary system: this was the complex tangle of war debts and reparations set up at the Peace *Reparations*

of Versailles in 1919. During the 1914–18 war, France and Britain had borrowed heavily from America. The Versailles Treaty had forced Germany to pay vast sums to her conquerors, and fixed the amount of debts owed. After massive inflation in postwar Germany, the 1924 Dawes Plan worked out a scheme of reparations better tailored to Germany's purse. But Germany still had to borrow to make the payments.

As one economist put it in 1929, "German industries, utilities and local governments had been borrowing in other countries far more than Germany had been paying out in cash. This made possible a formal transfer of the cash reparation payments [but] it meant merely that what she paid with one hand she borrowed with the other. This process could not continue much longer. It was uncertain how much more could safely be lent within Germany by foreigners. What had been lent was devoted very largely to restoring the working capital lost during the war, not to enlarging ultimate productive capacity. It had not yet led to any stable export surplus from Germany, and only by this means could Germany in the long run repay these borrowings, to say nothing of her reparation obligations. It was necessary, then, substantially to reduce German reparation obligations and to fix a total and a definite term of years to the annuities (77)." The Hague Conference, called in July, 1929, attempted to do just this.

After a month of talks at the Hague, the Young Plan was produced. It cut reparations from £125 to £100 millions. But "the only amount which under this new plan Germany unconditionally promises to transfer across her borders into foreign currencies is the relatively small one of 660 million marks a year . . . about $158 millions (78)." Philip Snowden returned from the Hague saying "it has been a strenuous time, but the Conference has raised our best hopes. The settlement of the reparations problem will give a feeling of security which is likely to help the economic reconstruction of Europe. The restoration of the political and economic sovereignty of Germany is one of the great achievements of the Conference (79)."

Young Plan (1929)

Hubert Henderson, Secretary of the Economic Advisory Council, questioned the value of the Young Plan. He told the Committee of Economists: "Few intelligent persons [feel] much

33

Opposite above German delegates attending the peace negotiations at Versailles in 1919; *opposite below* Parisians awaiting the distribution of German coal after France's seizure of the Ruhr coalfields in 1923

The Reparations Commission meeting in 1924 to assess Germany's ability to pay war debts.

confidence that Germany will in practice continue over two generations to make payments to other countries of the order of magnitude of £100 millions annually as the penalty of defeat in the last war (80)." Henderson's fears proved more realistic than Philip Snowden's optimism. Seven weeks later, on Black Thursday, 24th October, the Wall Street market collapsed.

Loans withdrawn   The most painful effect of the crash on the outside world was the sudden withdrawal of American loans from foreign capitals. Henderson later explained that "most countries in central and eastern Europe and Central and South America [had] been living with a balance of payments [which] was persistently and heavily adverse. The sums [which] they were liable to pay to other countries in respect of their imports, interest on loans, or in some cases for reparation obligations, greatly exceeded the sums that were due to them in respect of their exports. They had been meeting the difference by borrowing (81)."

As these loans had been made on a short-term basis, they could be recalled at any time. Keynes foresaw the situation during the pre-crash recession: "I take rather a grave view of possible

The poor of Vienna: *left* the free distribution of bread, and *right* taking
firewood from the Royal Forest

developments in the near future. For five years Germany has
[been] paying her way by borrowing . . . On account of the position in Wall Street her ability to borrow large sums has come to an
end. As a result of this her reserves have been melting away . . .
At the beginning of this year it was calculated that foreign bankers
had deposited something like $1,000 million in Berlin, recallable
at short notice. A withdrawal of 10 per cent of this sum would be
very inconvenient (82)."

Austria, too, had many short-term loans. *The Economist* *Austria*
reported from Vienna in November that "the position on the
money market and the poor prospects of raising a foreign loan
are resulting in very slow progress with the housing scheme . . .
Decline has been most marked in the stock exchange. All shares
are falling, even the best on the Vienna market, as the public has
become uneasy and is getting rid of its holdings (83)."

The loans on which the new prosperity of the Latin American *Latin*
countries depended also vanished overnight. "When the crisis *America*
came," wrote a correspondent of the *New York Times*, "this
artificial stimulus to business was suddenly removed. Additional

35

loans [could] not be secured (84)."

Europe   Large scale international lending had falsely boosted the unbalanced economies of the debtor nations. When the loans ended, the economist H. V. Hodson pointed out, "gold began to flow on a formidable scale from Germany and other countries which were in a weak position as regards the balance of international payments, towards countries in a strong position: of which the two outstanding cases were France and the United States (85)." *The Economist* described "the recurrence this summer of an influx of gold on a large scale to France (86)" and Hodson wrote in the *New Statesman* that "America, too, sits on a huge idle reserve of gold which she dare not use at home and will not invest abroad (87)." Maynard Keynes pointed out that, while the gold basis of the monetary system might have its virtues, it also brought dangers in times of economic disruption: "The return to the gold standard has been accompanied by a great increase in the world's demand for gold and by a bottling up of the greater part of the available surplus in the reserves of central banks (88)."

Every government struggled to hold onto its gold reserves. The hoarding and the withdrawal of loans caused a drastic reduction in international trade, which fell by one quarter between 1929 and 1932. "When the United States bubble was pricked, the U.S. capitalists cancelled orders for raw materials everywhere," wrote Walton Newbold, the editor of *The Social Democrat* (89). Agricultural countries who relied on exports were the first to feel the impact of the crash. An Australian correspondent wrote in July that, since the previous Autumn, Australia's "income has been appreciably reduced . . . The recent heavy decline in the prices of the chief exports, wool, wheat, meat, dairy produce and minerals have reduced the income from exports by perhaps £40 millions (90)." A newspaper report from Canada described Canada's "economic distress and unemployment," and explained that "Canada sows to wheat 24 million acres each year and is exploiting her forests and mineral resources on a scale far beyond the consuming capacity of her 10 million people. She must sell her primary products in world markets (91)."

Industrial nations hit   As their exports withered, the primary producing countries had no money to buy manufactured goods. Like nations with strong

Nazism in the streets of London (Hyde Park in the 1930s)

balances who tried to hoard their gold, they had to cut their imports from the industrial countries. Japan had trebled her silk production between 1914 and 1929, exporting most of it to America. Japan had no doubt provided the yarn for the silk stockings on the "thin spindly legs" dancing the Charleston described by Derek Patmore. But after the crash the export price of silk dropped by almost a third, and Japanese workers who had left the rice fields for the factories suddenly found themselves jobless. J. H. Thomas told the British Parliament in May, 1930, that "only last week . . . 935 factories had closed down" in Japan (92). Britain herself was especially vulnerable. As *The Economist* pointed out, Britain "lives by exchange to a greater extent than any other great country. Nearly thirty per cent in value of the goods and services produced in Great Britain are exported. The tragedy of unemployment remains in consequence of the reduced volume of world trade, and the small volume of commerce sailing the seas (93)."

The story repeated itself in South America. The new South American market developed by the United States and Britain now collapsed, as orders for raw materials were withdrawn at the same time as development loans. South American exports dropped by some forty per cent between 1929 and 1930. "Men engaged in public works construction were thrown out of employment and likewise many men engaged in the production of the basic articles for export. This meant business depression, declining wages, and unemployment," reported the *New York Times* in August, 1929 (94).

The fall in trade and exports forced producers to slash their prices. "During the last fifteen months," wrote Keynes in January, 1931, "the price level has plunged more and more steeply into the abyss . . . Most people . . . depend either on variable profits or on wages or salaries which will continue to be paid only if profits can be made by the employment of labour. A falling price level . . . tends to mean less profits, or none, and therefore less employment (95)."

European anxiety Europeans tried to make Americans more alive to the dangers of the situation than they seemed to be. A member of the International Chamber of Commerce reported to Washington that "it is claimed in Germany that, under present conditions . . . with the spectacular fall in prices [it] is actually more difficult for Germany to meet the lower Young Plan annuity than it was under former conditions to meet the higher Dawes plan annuity (96)." When Viscount D'Abernon, the English Ambassador in Berlin, broadcast in New York in the Spring of 1931, he told his listeners that "the present deplorable conditions are due in the main to the fall in the price of staple commodities. This fall has been brought about by adequate means of payment not being available. There has been a corner in gold and gold currency (97)."

President Hoover's own man in Germany was more pressing: "On May 7th our ambassador to Germany . . . arrived in Washington on an urgent mission. His purpose was to inform me that Chancellor of Germany Bruning had disclosed to him a detailed account of the disastrous financial crisis then developing in his country. Mr. Bruning had outlined the increasing economic strain, as shown by the flight of capital, currency difficulties, unemployment, drying up of credits from abroad (98)."

Austrian collapse Hoover was too late to do anything to help Austria. The desperate attempt of a customs union with Germany had not stopped her rapid slide to bankruptcy. Credit Anstalt, Austria's main bank, faced acute danger. On 30th May, 1931, an Austrian

A Black Market exchange of dollar notes in Berlin (1922)

correspondent wrote that "recent developments unfortunately suggest that the task of overcoming the difficulties under which this institution is labouring are proving more formidable than at one time seemed likely (99)." Next day, Credit Anstalt collapsed.

On 5th June President Hoover summoned his advisers to the White House in Washington. "I explained to them," he wrote in his memoirs, "that I felt the European situation had been degenerating much faster during the past month due to the failure of the Credit Anstalt . . . I had a definite proposal to lay before them . . . That was that we should postpone all collections of allied debts for one year in consideration of all the allies making similar postponements of reparations and all claims during the same period (100)." This was the famous Hoover Moratorium.

Hoover The Moratorium was announced to the world on 20th June,
Moratorium 1931. The English press commented on the 27th: "President
Hoover's plan for saving Germany [is] a supremely important
effort to avert a European catastrophe. He and those whom he had
consulted were moved to action not by pure philanthropy but by
enlightened self interest. They realized at last, what a great many
people on this side of the Atlantic had long been telling them,
that Germany was on the point of collapse which would mean a
stoppage, not merely of reparations, but of the interest on the
American money, amounting to some 300 millions sterling,
invested in the country (101)."

Whatever the motive, the Moratorium was a last minute
intervention to save Europe from continuing depression. "A week
ago Germany was in a critical condition faced with bankruptcy
and political upheaval . . . At the eleventh hour Mr. Hoover
offers a remedy which is good so far as it goes, as a temporary
relief or pick-me-up. We do not believe, and surely Mr. Hoover
himself cannot believe, that the postponement of debts will solve
the whole problem (102)."

Too late The move was in fact too late. By 30th June Germany owed
27 million marks, 12 million of which were on short term loans.
In July all the German banks collapsed. The pick-me-up had
failed.

4 Bankrupt Britain

THE 1920s did not bless Britain with the same wild prosperity as *British jobless* the United States. "The word written today on the hearts of British people, and graven on their minds is *unemployment*. For eight years, more than a million British workers, able and eager to work, have been denied the opportunity ... What a tragedy of human suffering; what a bankruptcy of statesmanship (103)."

These were the opening words of the Liberal Party pamphlet, *We Can Conquer Unemployment*, published during the election campaign of May, 1929. By then, as David Lloyd George the Liberal leader said, over a million Englishmen were out of work. Britain's dependence on her exports, and the overvaluation of the pound, had made her especially vulnerable to the dislocation of trade and to brakes on the free movement of gold. The Labour Party too, stressed that "unemployment is the master election issue of 1929 (104)."

The "bankrupt statesman" of Lloyd George's pamphlet was *Baldwin* Stanley Baldwin. Baldwin had been Conservative Prime Minister since 1925. He had done little to solve the mounting unemployment crisis. Indeed, he thought nothing could be done. Most economists believed that unemployment would force wages down, and lower production costs. This in turn would raise the demand for industrial products and so raise employment. In the long run all would be well. Keynes, however, realized that the system was not working: "In the long run we will all be dead," was his short reply. Influenced by Keynes, David Lloyd George advised the State to "lend its aid and, by a deliberate policy of national development, help to set going at full speed the great machinery of

41

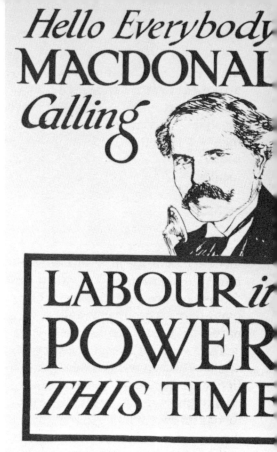

A Unionist poster (*left*) and a Labour poster (*right*) showing contrasting views of the Labour Party leader, Ramsay MacDonald, in the 1924 election

industry (105)."

Liberals seek expansion

The main idea of this Liberal scheme was to devise a large programme of public works to give work to the jobless. Keynes had taught Lloyd George that "every man put directly into employment leads to the secondary employment of yet another man (106)." Also, "if large sums of government money can be poured out quickly for the erection of public buildings and other types of construction this [will] put numbers of men at work supplying the materials or doing the actual work of building. These men will spend their wages for food, clothing and shelter. The retail trades will prosper accordingly, and so on (107)." This was the so-called multiplier theory. Keynes realized that inadequate personal spending power, causing inadequate demand, was a root-cause of the depression.

But the Keynesian ideas in Lloyd George's Liberal manifesto mystified the Conservative and Labour leaders. "Is this the moment," asked the Conservative, Baldwin, "to gamble with rash socialist schemes of state control [which] would not give employment to half of the present unemployed, and which would increase the cost of living, owing to the enormous loans that would have to be raised? (108)." The Labour Party showed a similar ignorance of the expansionist ideas behind the Liberal schemes. Lloyd George had proposed that "the whole expenditure . . . should be met out of loans, and he pretends that his entire plan can be carried into effect without adding one penny to the rates or taxes . . . But the public is well aware that if it does not pay today it will have to pay tomorrow . . . Wise men shove such things into the waste-paper basket without more ado (109)."

The Labour electoral victory of 1929 was followed by a fortunate, if short, revival of trade. Hubert Henderson, Secretary of the Economic Advisory Council, wrote in April that "the buoyant conditions of the American and European stock markets gave rise to repercussions immediately favourable to business activity . . . no serious world depression made itself felt until the Wall Street collapse (110)." *Elections of 1929*

Before the crash a weakness in the British economy had been spotlighted by the Hatry scandal. Clarence Hatry, a slot-machine manufacturer, had begun forging stock certificates for investment trusts. In September, *The Economist* said that Hatry's arrest "marked the final collapse of an ambitious financial edifice . . . The speculative boom of the last two years has revealed a number of abuses (111)."

The great Wall Street crash of October reduced confidence still more. "For hours after the Stock Exchange had closed this afternoon there were hundreds of stockbrokers and clerks congregating in Shooters Court off Throgmorton Street, or rushing between there and their offices in pouring rain, for New York's slump had its importance to the Stock Exchange here (112)." Hubert Henderson noted that "a severe world-wide trade depression has been superimposed on our special national difficulties

(113)." Unemployment began to rise again until by March, 1930, 1,700,000 people were out of work.

Here was the problem facing Ramsay MacDonald's Labour government. One of MacDonald's colleagues, J. H. Thomas, was to be "reserved for the special task of co-ordinating all schemes for the relief of unemployment (114)." J. H. Thomas believed, like Henderson, that "the heart of this problem is the long-continued depression of some of our leading exporting industries . . . There attaches accordingly to industries like coal and cotton a large surplus of labour which we have not yet succeeded in absorbing in other occupations (115)."

State and industry Thomas therefore tried to fight unemployment by rationalizing industry. He told the Cabinet that he would try "to attack the problem of unemployment at its roots, by openly abandoning the bad old policy of laissez-faire and thus bringing the government into a new relationship with industry (116)."

By May, 1930, Thomas could tell the House of Commons that "there is not a leader of trade, commerce or labour in this country who, either individually or collectively, I have not met during the last twelve months . . . I believe the industrial future of this country, with all that it means as far as unemployment is concerned, will never be solved by any government unless that government can carry with them [the] hearty co-operation of those engaged in industry (117)."

But Thomas's "rationalization" was not taken to its logical socialist conclusion. True, the Cabinet discussed "taking some steps to modernize industry, including if necessary, the acquisition by the government of further powers (118)." But Labour policy involved no clear idea of public ownership and no real understanding of a managed economy. When studies of the cotton and steel industries recommended financial reorganization, mergers, or modern machinery, Thomas refused to force the issue and impose them on the industrialists. Surely the depression would right itself in the end? Industrial co-operation would help. Government intervention on Keynesian lines was unnecessary.

Mosley's policy By early 1930 Thomas's policy had made no impact on the slump. Sir Oswald Mosley, one of Thomas's lieutenants, wrote a memorandum suggesting what to do. "The Government through-

King George V (reigned 1910–36)

out have pinned their hopes to rationalization," he told the House of Commons. "The theory is, that if we can restore our export trade by rationalization to its previous position in the markets of the world, we shall absorb our present unemployed . . . The hope of recovering our position through an expansion of our export trade is a dangerous illusion . . . It is to the *home* market that we must look [and] if we are to build up a home market it must be agreed that this nation must to some extent be insulated from the electric shocks of present world conditions (119)."

In other words, Mosley wanted import controls behind which the home industry could be built up. He was influenced by Keynes, who saw that trade, like employment, sometimes needed the

Government to step in. Mosley argued his proposals in Cabinet:

Mosley: "It is a complete fallacy that when you have rationalized the basic industries you'll have solved the problem."

MacDonald: "Is there no future for this country, then?"

Mosley: "We must rationalize to hold our position at all ... This country, if it is to survive at present standard of life, has got to be isolated from other countries. The high purchasing power of the home population is the only solution (120)."

Mosley wanted to achieve this by putting men to work. A vast plan of public works to be financed by borrowing was his second main idea. As *The Times* reported, Mosley suggested that "a £100 million programme of the Unemployment Grants Committee [the Government agency for administering funds] and a £100 million road programme should be concentrated into three years (121)." The Government did accept the need for some public works, but Thomas told the Cabinet that "to sanction large expenditure just to provide work temporarily for X thousand men would be foolish. Indeed by doing so we might do much more harm than good in the effect of such a policy upon the cost of our production (122)."

Labour rejects expansion Thomas failed to understand the Keynesian multiplier theory behind Mosley's schemes. The proposed means of paying for the public works was liked by the Government even less than their extent. Such huge loans would unbalance the budget. To financiers of the old school the balanced budget was all important. Government spending must always be met by taxation, in order to offset increased purchasing power. To pay through borrowing was inflationary; and it would place an extra burden on the shoulders of future generations. The Keynesian view, shared by Mosley, was that to finance extra spending through borrowing would not be inflationary if idle resources were used to meet the extra demand.

However, as Mosley wrote: "The loan method, or deficit financing, during a depression shocked to the very core the financial orthodoxy of this socialist administration (123)." The Chancellor of the Exchequer, Philip Snowden, saw himself, as *The Times* did, as "the unbending guardian of the public purse (124)" with the sacred trust of balancing the budget. Oswald Mosley's views were heretical. Mosley's "programme has been rejected," wrote *The Economist*, "on the grounds that the additional money cannot be found [and] that the loans of the magnitude proposed required for his public works are impossible today (125)."

So, on 20th May, Mosley resigned. A meeting of Mosley's supporters at Cliveden was described by the diarist, Harold Nicolson: "The main conclusion is that Parliament, though susceptible to dealing with politics is hopeless at finance and economics . . . that we are about to enter the worst crisis in our history . . . Tom Mosley tells me that he will shortly launch [his] National Party (126)." Placards were soon posted everywhere, inviting recruits for the New Party, and proposing remedies for unemployment:

> Action not Faction!
> Stop playing politics
> Reform Parliament
> Re-build trade
> Control imports
> Keep up wages
> Get to work on the Mosley plan.
>
> The Old Parties have Failed!
> Get to work on the Mosley Plan
> Tories don't care
> Liberals aren't there
> Labour doesn't dare
> Clear out the old gang
> Keep up wages.

Meanwhile Thomas had had to tell the Commons that more and more people were being thrown out of work. "I, least of all, will minimize the figures. I do not attempt to minimize them. They are rising (127)." In July, they had risen to two millions, by December to two and a half millions. The Prime Minister, Ramsay Mac-Donald, himself took charge of the problem. MacDonald was defeatist in his new role, as he admitted in Cabinet: "Can we find work and take people off the register? As to building [we] are up against a blank wall. Agriculture, we are not sure how to handle the problem apart from land drainage (128)." MacDonald blamed the capitalist system for the slump. At the Labour Party Conference he told members: "We are not on trial; it is the system

47

The horrors of the slump: an unemployed man and his family outside
their London shack in 1932

under which we live. It has broken down, not only in this little
island; it has broken down in Europe, in Asia, in America; it has
broken down everywhere as it was bound to break down (129)."
Many Labour supporters already believed that capitalism was the
cause of unemployment; they scarcely expected a minority Government to tackle the root of the evil.

Cost of relief   "All that is possible is to keep people standing by, and use the
Insurance Fund," said MacDonald in Cabinet (130). The Govern-
ment plunged deeper and deeper into debt as it paid out more in
benefits. The whole time it was attacked for the rising deficit and
for abuses of the system. Margaret Bondfield, Minister of Labour,
told the House of Commons that "the debt of the Unemployment
Fund on May 24th, 1930 was £41 millions (131)." Next month she
admitted in Cabinet that even "Footballers are getting the dole.
Employers are using the fund as a dovetailing device (132)."

A mobile coffee stall serving the hungry and homeless during the Depression

Lloyd George bitterly attacked the Labour Government's priorities: "We are borrowing £40 million to pay the dole [and] we are borrowing nothing for the purpose of providing work . . . If the tasks which the Government are asked to undertake were not beneficial to the community, then it would be a perfect waste to spend money on them. But nobody says that . . . Is it not therefore very much better that it should be done when you have 2,250,000 unemployed than that you should wait until the turn of the tide . . .? You save the money you are borrowing in order to pay these allowances, and you put the men on to work (133)."

But "the Cabinet examined the extent of the relief works which they had initiated, and which were generally agreed to be as large as they should be in existing circumstances (134)." The Chancellor stuck firmly to the Treasury's view that public works had to pay for themselves and not involve too much Government borrowing. MacDonald accepted the Ministry of Transport's practical arguments, as well as Treasury theory. The Cabinet heard from the Ministry that Britain did not need more roads than those already planned.

Having rejected Mosley's Keynesian economics, the Government under MacDonald's defeatist lead tried to end the depression by conventional means. During the election campaign of 1930 MacDonald had proposed "the raising of the school age with necessary maintenance grants" as one way of curing unemployment. "We must dam the influx of premature people into industry (135)." A year later the President of the Board of Education reminded his leader of his promise: "Our Party are asking: what are we doing about unemployment? The larger part of them continue to regard the raising of the school age as a material part of our policy, and at this desperate juncture not to try to insist upon passing the Bill would seem to them to be deliberately throwing over one of the possible means of alleviating unemployment (136)." But even this orthodox measure was put off for financial reasons.

The problem of the depressed cities was now taken up. Thomas told his Cabinet colleagues that "the problem of attracting new industrial enterprises to the depressed areas [is] now being carefully examined." But it was shelved. Thomas explained that "many of the depressed areas, notably the coal mining valleys of South Wales, are quite unsuitable for any other industries (137)."

During the unemployment debate in December, 1930, MacDonald's Government was bitterly attacked for its meagre efforts. Winston Churchill declared: "We have had about twenty days of these unemployment debates in the present year . . . They have produced no results . . . nothing effective will be done in the present parliament . . . That is the one solid conclusion which emerges from all the debates (138)."

While the lives of the unemployed were grim, even those with work were hit; for the Government tried to cut wages in the old hope of lowering prices to increase output. In 1931, the economist G. D. H. Cole wrote that "demands for wage reductions are now pouring thick and fast upon the Trades Unions . . . The railwaymen are restive under the reductions which they accepted recently, the miners are pressing their demand for a guaranteed minimum wage . . . the chemical workers have been faced with a general demand for reductions (139)." Cole pointed out, as Keynes had done, that cuts in wages only reduced purchasing power. "The

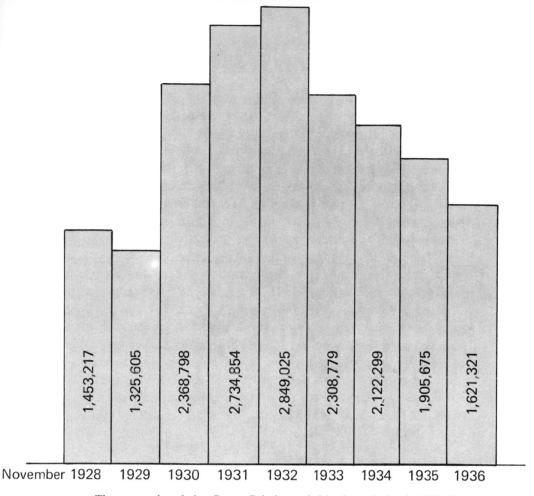

November 1928	1929	1930	1931	1932	1933	1934	1935	1936
1,453,217	1,325,605	2,368,798	2,734,854	2,849,025	2,308,779	2,122,299	1,905,675	1,621,321

The unemployed in Great Britain and Northern Ireland 1928–36:
above the total number of registered unemployed; *below* a graph showing
the high percentage of unemployed to the total registered working
population

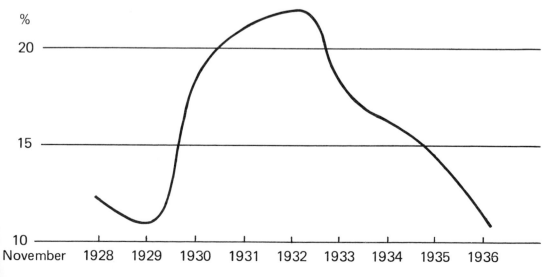

game of wage reductions is not worth the candle." Oswald Mosley pursued his attack in the Commons: "The method of saving the country is not only to cut down but to build up . . . These suggestions to put the nation in bed on a starvation diet are the suggestions of an old woman in a fright (140)."

Economy Committee

MacDonald's Government grew more and more frightened as the unemployment figure soared toward three millions. Then, in the summer, the European banks collapsed. The main German bank failed on 13th July. On 31st July, the May Economy Committee, created in March "to make recommendations to the Chancellor of the Exchequer for effecting forthwith all possible reductions in national expenditure," published its Report. As *The Times* said, this Report "revealed the prospect of a Budget deficit next year of £120 millions (141)." The Report also recommended economies of £97 millions, including a 20 per cent cut in unemployment benefits. All the Government did was to set up an Economy Committee to report on the May report. Then it broke up for the summer holidays.

The Economy Report was over-pessimistic. But it certainly increased the loss of sterling from London, a loss already serious after the European bank collapse. Foreign governments panicked at the frightening forecast.

Drain on sterling

The heavy drain on sterling by foreign bankers continued. As MacDonald later explained to the Commons: "Between 13th July and 30th July the Bank lost £34 millions in gold. Temporary credits were arranged to supplement that loss in order to save gold . . . By the third week in August these were practically exhausted (142)." Something urgently had to be done to restore confidence. The Economy Committee suggested a compromise 10 per cent cut in unemployment benefits. Attacking the idea of balancing the budget, Keynes wrote: "My own policy, so long as the slump lasts, would be to continue to borrow for the Unemployment Fund and to impose a revenue tariff (143)."

The Chancellor of the Exchequer, Philip Snowden, wanted unemployment benefits cut, and adamantly opposed tariffs. Ramsay MacDonald was ready to use either method. But the Trade Unions angrily protested against a cut in benefits.

The Labour Government insisted upon balancing the budget,

yet drew away from the old means of balancing it—by benefit cuts. *Labour*
They also rejected Keynes' new idea of tariffs. In any case, the *Government*
loan needed to restore confidence in sterling, and stop all reserves *split*
draining away, was made conditional by the New York bankers on
cuts in unemployment benefits. As MacDonald said later, the
Government "had to do not one, but two things. It had to balance
its budget, or take steps to secure a balanced budget, and to put its
unemployment finance on a sound financial basis (144)."

On 23rd August "a minority of the Cabinet opposed the 10 per
cent cut. The majority held that the Government could only
adopt this proposal if there was complete or almost complete
unanimity in the Cabinet. Everybody agreed that the position was
such that it was impossible to continue (145)." MacDonald
accordingly had an audience with King George V. *The Times*
Parliamentary correspondent wrote: "The Prime Minister's
friends believed on Sunday night that he would resign office
(146)." But next day, Buckingham Palace issued a portentous
communiqué to the press: "His Majesty the King invited the
Prime Minister [MacDonald], Mr. Stanley Baldwin, and Sir
Herbert Samuel to Buckingham Palace this morning, and the
formation of a National Government is under consideration."
The economic crisis had caused the gravest political crisis seen in
England for many years.

The formation of the National Government (25th August, *Coalition*
1931)—a coalition—brought a short breathing space in the midst
of the crisis. Philip Snowden, who remained Chancellor of the Exchequer, was one of the few Ministers to follow Ramsay Mac-
Donald into the new Government. He described later how "the
plans which we announced for balancing the Budget had the
immediate effect of restoring confidence. For some days the strain of
withdrawals fell sharply and we hoped that it might dry up (147)."

MacDonald believed he had taken the only action possible to
avert financial collapse. He wrote personally to every Labour
Member of Parliament: "I have consulted every shade of opinion
and given the situation the most careful thought of which I am
capable. It is clear that in the midst of the world depression
[fears] have arisen abroad as to the stability of our credit [and]
it was therefore absolutely necessary to have the loan from the

Mass unemployed hunger marchers in Trafalgar Square (London, 1932)

New York bankers (148)."

MacDonald's justifications were echoed by a leading American journalist, Walter Lipmann, writing in the *New York Herald Tribune*: "At the beginning of August Britain was sliding down the steep incline towards national bankruptcy . . . The worst effects are suffered by those who can bear them least: by old people with little pensions or little savings, by wage-earners and salaried people . . . I can well understand that when Ramsay MacDonald looked into such an abyss of agony opening up before his people he knew he must act first and explain afterwards (149)."

Labour rejects
MacDonald
But the Labour Party did not accept such explanations of their leader's action. Nearly the whole of the Labour Party deserted MacDonald, and went over into opposition. Their new leader George Lansbury declared at Kilmarnock: "I have always denied that there was any financial crisis . . . I deny that the wealth of this country was being drained away. What happened was that the moneylenders of the City of London had got themselves into

an infernal tangle and could not get out without the assistance of the State (150)."

"The crisis was real, not an invention (151)," replied Arthur Greenwood, another Labour ex-minister. Arthur Greenwood was one minister to have opposed the cuts in benefits. Not only had the crisis not been overcome, it was still only too real. For the formation of the National Government not only cost MacDonald the support of his Party; it failed to improve Britain's finances for more than a few weeks. Philip Snowden brought in an economy budget and cut the pay of all state employees. "The great national crisis," said the Socialist writer Beatrice Webb scornfully, "has led to all sorts of disaster to the wage earners of Great Britain, from cuts in the unemployment benefit, and cuts in the pay of the soldiers and the sailors, [to] economies in the education of our children (152)."

But the run on sterling continued; the £80 million loan from New York had not revived foreign confidence. Philip Snowden told the House of Commons that calls for inflation had had "a most damaging effect. There was political uncertainty, and the news of the unrest that occurred in the Navy was recorded in scare headlines in every foreign newspaper (153)." The Chancellor was referring to the sailors' mutiny at Invergordon, staged in anger at their pay cut. *Invergordon mutiny*

Confidence was shattered by the Invergordon mutiny, "If England can no longer trust to her naval crews, how can she ever be sure of the morrow or safeguard her power in the world? (154)." Panic among bankers spread like a forest fire. On 18th September the drain on Treasury credits was £18 millions. Snowden told the Commons that he had "no alternative but to suspend the gold convertibility of the currency." Britain was off the gold standard.

Catastrophe had arrived. In London, posters said to be printed by the Co-operative Movement showed a scene of the Battle of Jutland over the caption: "The British Navy at Jutland in 1916 beat the ex-Kaiser, and at Invergordon in 1931 it beat Mr. Montagu Norman" (Governor of the Bank of England). But nothing terrible happened and general resentment was felt among Labour ex-Ministers that "nobody told us we could do this (155)."

At the Political Magician's Dinner. *The Man Above*: "They're all very funny tricks, but where's the magician who can produce some work?"

(1931)

All party leaders had believed, like the classical economists, that the gold standard would automatically ensure a healthy balance of payments; too many imports would lead to a squeeze until the situation righted itself. But when automatic controls proved useless the Tories demanded an election, confident they would win under the umbrella of a National Government. Ramsay MacDonald, expelled from the Labour party, was forced to agree to an election. He asked the electorate for a blank cheque, or a "doctor's mandate," as he called it, to deal with the crisis.

Elections   Ramsay MacDonald's explusion had embittered the feelings between the (Parliamentary) Labour Opposition and the (National) Labour Party. The 1931 election did so still more. In a dramatic radio broadcast, Philip Snowden declared: "In front of me, as part of the wireless arrangement, is a red light; and a red

"Putting the cart before the horse" (David Low). The government put its expensive social programme before the basic problem of massive unemployment

light is a warning of dangers to be avoided. I am going to give you this warning tonight . . . My late colleagues in the Labour Government hadn't the courage to face the unpopularity which necessary measures of economy would naturally meet with . . . I hope you have read the election programmes of the Labour Party . . . This is not socialism. It is Bolshevism run mad (156)."

The National Government swept to power with a massive majority of 521 seats, 473 of them Conservative. The Conservative party leader, Lord Stonehaven, claimed that the coalition had "a mandate to carry out Tory policy (157)." Ramsay MacDonald complained to Snowden: "When the National Government is mentioned, a Tory government is implied (158)." MacDonald was in effect the Labour leader of a Conservative Government.

National Government

57

This Government was to rule the country, first under his leadership and then under Stanley Baldwin and Neville Chamberlain, until the outbreak of the Second World War in 1939. Oswald Mosley's extreme right-wing ideas failed to win his New Party a single seat at the election; but the spectre of fascism darkened British life for a decade.

Economic problems loomed over everything. The British electorate had voted for the National Government believing that only a coalition could do the job. Nearly three million people were now out of work.

Import duties   The National Government's first answer was protection. Import tariffs to protect the home market had been the basis of the Conservative electoral platform. Neville Chamberlain, the new Chancellor of the Exchequer, now introduced a 10 per cent Imports Duty Bill.

This was announced "to a House of Commons whose floor and galleries were packed with an attentive and illustrious audience. The importance of the occasion was rightly recognized, for it constituted the definite beginning of the practical work for which the National Government was created (159)."

Chamberlain was exuberant in his claims for his Bill. Tariffs would produce more work, smaller unemployment benefits, higher tax revenues, and a balanced budget; more exports and so a proper balance of payments. A *Spectator* correspondent observed: "For better or worse this country has departed from the Free Trade System that served it so long and so well (160)."

Trade protection was made possible by departure from the gold standard. The old system had failed; the Government itself must now control the economy. Devaluation and tariffs were two ways in which the National Government set about this task. In April, Neville Chamberlain proposed a third method, "a new account to be called the Exchange Equalization Account. I propose to ask powers to borrow up to £150 millions for this account . . . If we are to avoid violent and perilous fluctuations in our currency, especially those which are due to speculative operations [we must] hold adequate reserves in order that we may meet any sudden withdrawal of capital, and check and repel these speculative movements (161)."

When Britain went off the Gold Standard in 1931 many people obtained
good prices for articles of gold

The Minister of Agriculture echoed this theme with an Agricultural Marketing Bill: "We must seek to establish an equilibrium of
price levels. We must ask ourselves what that level is to be. Is it to
be determined by the lowest cost of the most favourably situated
producers? That was the solution of the nineteenth century . . .
We have to deal with the twentieth century (162)." This Bill was
yet another example of how the economy could be managed by
the Government. It answered the Liberal Clement Davies's
complaint that "today we are suffering from defective and
antiquated methods of marketing. Consequently there is no fixed
national price. Prices are fixed haphazardly and the country
suffers (163)." The Bill provided for "regulating the importation
and sale of agricultural products and for organizing the production of secondary agricultural products (164)."

The National Government did not only rely, as J. H. Thomas
had done, on the Victorian staple industries of coal, textiles and
shipbuilding to boost trade and employment. The President of
the Board of Trade drew attention "to the new industries which
have come to this country . . . They include businesses like knit-
wear, ribbons, furnishing fabrics and other textiles, clothing,
electric radio apparatus, leather goods, toilet products, paper
(165)."

Investment in these new businesses was helped by the Government's policy of cheap money, and low interest rates on borrowed
capital. The same policy helped the housing boom. George
Orwell, who published his novels during these years, wrote:
"You know how these streets fester all over the inner-outer
suburbs. Always the same, long, long rows of little semi-detached
houses, the stucco front, the privet hedge, the green front door.
The Laurels, the Myrtles, the Hawthorns, Mon Repos, Belle Vue
(166)."

People could buy their new houses, furniture, radios and
clothes while prices were kept down. Even those without work
were helped to do so by the growth of hire purchase. Orwell
pointed out that "in a decade of unparalleled depression, the
consumption of all cheap luxuries had increased. The two things
that have probably made the greatest difference of all are the
movies and the mass-production of cheap smart clothes . . . The
youth who leaves school at fourteen [is] out of work at twenty
[but] for two pounds ten on the hire-purchase system he can buy
himself a suit . . . The girl can look like a fashion plate at an even
lower price. You may have three-halfpence in your pocket and
not a prospect in the world, and only the corner of a leaky bed-
room to go home to; but in your new clothes you can stand on the
street corner indulging in a private day-dream of yourself as
Clark Gable or Greta Garbo, which compensates you for a great
deal (167)."

As tariffs, quotas, subsidies and a regulated cheap money
policy followed devaluation, the Government seemed to be
meddling in every aspect of life. The same criticism was made
of President Roosevelt's New Deal. The era of laissez-faire was
over. Books appeared with titles like *Modern Government as a*

"Spend for Employment:" the idea of expansion frightened orthodox economists during the Depression

Busybody in Other Men's Matters, Bureaucracy Triumphant, or *The New Despotism.* In the long run, management was the right answer to the problems of the depression, and the best way to prevent another slump: it led to the managed economy generally accepted in every capitalist country today.

Its short-term success was less evident. The advantages of the exchange fund and of devaluation fell away when other countries (the United States in 1933 and France in 1936) followed suit. Neville Chamberlain himself admitted in 1933: "I had estimated that I should receive from the new Tariff Duties £32 millions ... In the end the actual revenue I received was just under £22 millions (168)." In seeking to balance the budget, his restrictive economies had cancelled out some of the good effects of his tariffs, subsidies and cheap money.

Chamberlain's economies included the pruning of local *Deflation* authority spending. State-aided schemes were out. Kingsley

Women marching from Derby to London in 1934 in protest against their
unemployment

Martin wrote cynically of the National Government's economies, and of its trivial efforts to fight unemployment: "The discussion [about] whether it is more patriotic to save or to spend reminds me of [a] Cambridge Don. He was seriously troubled about unemployment . . . He had thought of three things he could do. He was having his rooms redecorated; he was having his bed lengthened as it was at present uncomfortably short; thirdly, he was having a silver egg-cup made because Cambridge eggs were unusually large (169)."

Hardship   At first the Government's policies did little to give work to the jobless. In February, 1932, *The Times* reported "a rise in the unemployment figures of 218,490 in one month, bringing the total to 2,728,411 (170)." In June, the Cabinet heard the Minister of Labour speak of "the prospective unemployment situation, intimating [that] we were likely to be faced with a volume of unemployment next winter greater than anything experienced previously (171)." And in September, *The Economist* reported that "according to the figures issued by the Minister of Labour last week [the] unemployment figure was 2,859,828 (172)."

"The average unemployed family lives on an income of round about thirty shillings a week, of which at least a quarter goes in rent," wrote Orwell (173). A correspondent explained that, when the 10 per cent cut in benefits was made, "a duration of six months was imposed. Further, those applicants who had not paid thirty contributions in two years ceased to be entitled to any benefit at all. A new form of state aid was created for all [who] were thus excluded from benefit. It was [to be] drawn, not as a right, but only in proportion to the ascertained need of the applicant. Hence the so-called Means Test (174)." Its aim, like the brake on public building, was to cut local authority spending. "At least £25 millions must have been saved to the Exchequer in the year," he added.

The Means Test resurrected the old Victorian Poor Law idea, *Means Test* with its deadening psychological effect. George Orwell wrote, "The thing that horrified and amazed me was to find that many . . . were *ashamed* of being unemployed. The middle classes were still talking about 'lazy idle loafers on the dole' and naturally these opinions percolated to the working class themselves (175)." And J. B. Priestley, the Yorkshire novelist, saw "men who, though they knew they were idle and useless through no fault of their own, felt defeated and somewhat tainted. Their self respect was shredding away (176)."

The guilt and fear of the "dole mentality" was heightened by the workings of the Means Test. Nobody felt secure under the anomalies and whims of the new local committees which made the payments. Disability pensions and workmen's compensation were often noted in the assessment of need. MacDonald wrote to Philip Snowden: "I am quite certain that the policy of local Public Assistance Committees is anything but wise or just (177)." His son Malcolm told him that "the administration of the Means Test [is] doing us harm and there are undoubtedly many hard cases (178)."

ORDINARY BENEFIT

Age	Males		Females	
	Old rate	New rate	Old rate	New rate
16	6/–	5/6	5/–	4/6
17	9/–	8/–	7/6	6/9
18–20	14/–	12/6	12/–	10/9
21–65	17/–	15/3	15/–	13/6

Above Unemployment Benefit Rates in Britain (1931): the Unemployment Insurance Order of 8th October, 1931 (National Government) introduced a 10 per cent cut which the Labour government had refused to make. The rate of additional benefit for an adult dependent was reduced from nine to eight shillings per week; the rate for a child remained at the old rate of two shillings. On 26th July, 1934, the benefits were raised again to the pre-1931 rate, and on 31st October 1935 the child's rate was increased to three shillings. *Below* a table showing the number of false claims for benefits (1931–33)

	1931	1932	1933
Fined	805	1,247	1,433
Imprisoned	304	388	343
Bound over	69	150	115
Summons dismissed	50	91	111
Summons withdrawn	8	30	15
Adjourned sine die	–	3	–
	1,236	1,909	2,017

A sufferer described his own hardship in 1934 when he failed to find a job after his engineering firm had closed down: "My wife was able to earn a few shillings to supplement our dole income [and] the feeling of strain became more marked. The final blow came when the Means Test was put into operation . . . Both my wife and son, who had just commenced to earn a few shillings, told me to get out, as I was living on them and taking the food they needed (179)." In the same way, George Orwell described how "the most cruel effect of the Means Test is the way in which it breaks up families. An old age pensioner if a widower would live with one of his children. Under the Means Test, however, he counts as a 'lodger' and if he stays at home his children's dole will be docked (180)."

Action came in 1934 with Neville Chamberlain's Unemployment Act. This ended the anomalies by introducing central state control. A new Unemployment Assistance Board was given the task of handing out relief. Relief was no longer "dole," but "assistance."

Meanwhile, J. B. Priestley wrote, "The England of the dole did *Poverty* not seem to me a pleasant place. We could not be proud of its creation (181)." Walter Greenwood described the "streets, mazes, jungles of tiny houses cramped and huddled together [in] some cases only one room 'alow and one aloft; public houses by the score where forgetfulness lurks in a mug, pawnshops by the dozen where you can raise the wind to buy forgetfulness (182)." The high streets of the towns were dotted with pubs and pawnshops as well as hire purchase shops and cinemas. And just off the high streets J. B. Priestley saw "a warren of people living in wretched conditions in miserable huddles of mean streets and dirty little houses (183)."

The titles of a series of articles in *The Daily Herald* cried out for action: "Slum clearance a Social duty!"—"A Shame which must be removed!"—"Begin anywhere, but begin! (184)." But the Government was slow to start. Thomas Jones tried to use his influence with Baldwin. He told his daughter: "I used the example of Mussolini and Rome and urged a vigorous clearing out of London slums . . . He agrees but will not act either at Cabinet or by sending for the Minister in charge (185)." Walter de la Mare's poem, *The Slum Child*, remained true (186):

> In leafless Summer's stench and noise
> I'd sit and play
> With other as lean-faced girls and boys
> And sticks and stones for toys.
>
> Then up the noisome stairs I'd creep
> For food and rest
> Or empty bellied, lie and weep
> My silly woes to sleep.
>
> What evil and filth and poverty
> In childhood harboured me.

The slums were worst in the "distressed areas" where families were dependent upon the old industries, those hardest hit by the depression. In the Spring of 1932 a Member of Parliament said that "for the first three months in this year, compared with the first three months of last year, I find that there are 50,000 fewer miners employed in the coal mining industry (187)." The mining town of Merthyr in 1934 had an unemployment rate of sixty per cent. Lancashire dependended on her cotton industry. J. B. Priestley described how "the whole district had been tied to prosperity, to its very existence, with threads of cotton; and you can hear them snapping all the time . . . Nobody has any money to buy, rent or run mills any more . . . The tales of men driven out of business were innumerable. I heard of one former cotton king who was seen picking up cigarette ends in the street (188)".

The *Manchester Guardian* reported that "we have made no comparable progress with the problem of the derelict areas. Those men who have been unemployed for anything from five to ten years have given up any hope of getting back to work. They regard themselves [as] just a waste product of the economic process [and] the majority just drift (189)."

The jobless   The poet Stephen Spender described this drifting of the unemployed (190):

> Moving through the silent crowd
> Who stand behind dull cigarettes
> These men who idle in the road,
> I have the sense of falling light.

They lounge at corners of the street
And greet friends with a shrug of shoulder
And turn their empty pockets out,
The cynical gestures of the poor.

I'm haunted by these images,
I'm haunted by their emptiness.

In *The Road to Wigan Pier*, George Orwell noted the effects on health of bad diet. "In Sheffield, you have the feeling of walking among a population of troglodytes . . . the most obvious sign of under-nourishment is the badness of everybody's teeth . . . Even the children's teeth have a frail bluish appearance which means, I suppose, calcium deficiency. Several dentists have told me that in industrial districts a person over thirty with any of his or her own teeth is coming to be an abnormality." And in London, "It was impossible, looking about one then, not to be struck by the physical degeneracy of modern England . . . Puny limbs, sickly faces, under the weeping London sky!"

Orwell underlines one of the great paradoxes of life in the same book: "You may shiver all night for lack of bedclothes, but in the morning you can go to the public library and read the news that has been telegraphed for your benefit from San Francisco and Singapore. Twenty million people are underfed but literally everyone in England has access to a radio. Whole sections of the working class who have been plundered of all they really need are being compensated, in part, by cheap luxuries which mitigate the surface of life."

The unemployed joined mass hunger marches in protest at the Government's failure to find them work. Ellen Wilkinson described how on the way to canvass the Prime Minister "we had a walk of nine miles in face of the gale. There were enough police and detectives to have kept us in check if we had been bandits (191)." In October, 1936, came the great Jarrow march southward to London. In Hyde Park, "the Communist Party had gathered a big demonstration on a general unemployment protest [which] grew to enormous size when it was known that the Jarrow crusaders were there (192)."

Unemployment had strengthened the English Communist

Hunger marches

67

Unemployed men scratch for pieces of unwanted coal on a slag heap in Newcastle

Party. Social conscience also led many intellectuals, including Stephen Spender, to adopt Marxist ideas. There was a general growth of leftist feeling. Robert Graves said that, amongst undergraduates, "the test of being 'advanced' was no longer whether one understood modernist poems, but whether one understood Marxism. A magazine founded at Cambridge in 1932, *Cambridge Left*, published Marxian analyses of literature and poems about the class struggle (193)."

But the Communists, like Mosley's Fascists, won no seats in

The headquarters of the British Union of Fascists in London

Parliament during the depression; neither extremist Party was a danger, as in Germany or Italy, to the parliamentary system itself. Marxists in Britain, as in France, had learned from the German example that, if the State was allowed to "wither away" according to their doctrine, the result might be a Fascist dictatorship instead of a Communist utopia. In France, the Communists eventually joined the Popular Front. In Britain, too, revolution was not on the cards. Discontent was siphoned off by demonstrations and marches. The moderate National Government continued to

Extremists lack support

69

govern moderately. The depression had at least forced them to break with outdated pre-war attitudes; laissez-faire had given way to the all-important concept of economic management.

Brighter hopes Unemployment did not drop below two millions until 1935. But Neville Chamberlain could claim in 1934 that "the volume of our industrial production has very much gone up and equilibrium has practically been restored in the balance of payments . . . If you look to the unemployment figures and statistics of retail trade, iron and steel production and house building, in every case you see a definite revival of activity . . . I would say that we have now finished the story of *Bleak House* and that we are sitting down this afternoon to enjoy the first chapter of *Great Expectations* (194)."

5 Europe in Revolution

OF ALL the nations in Western Europe, Germany was the worst hit by the depression. The main Berlin bank, the Darmstaedter and National, failed on 13th July, 1931. All other banks in Germany shut down for the time being. A London journalist reported from Berlin on 17th July that "the run on the savings banks started early this morning [and] long queues had formed even before opening time. But only sums that were needed for wages, salaries, taxes and other essential payments were handed over the counter. There was a good deal of wrangling and arguing (195)." Bank failures meant, first, that depositors lost their savings, and second that many firms went bankrupt when loans were suddenly called in. For both these reasons, many people lost their jobs.

Thousands of Germans were thrown out of work when the full force of the American recession was felt. Hubert Henderson wrote that "the resultant pressure on the German economic system reached an acute stage in 1930 (196)." J. H. Thomas reported in the House of Commons during a debate on the German crisis that "in February of this year, their unemployment figure was 3,365,000, a million higher than five months ago (197)."

The following Spring the head of American Express in Berlin, O. G. Villard, told his friend Ramsay MacDonald: "The industrial situation gets worse. They are now well over the five million mark in unemployment. Yesterday I had a long talk with Kummer [who is] one of the leaders of the Metal Workers' Union. He tells me that the Union leaders have come to the conclusion that for many years to come the normal unemployment, if one may use such a term, will be around three million persons. This is a desper-

A Communist Parade in Berlin (1926): Hitler threatened the German people with the prospect of Bolshevism

ate outlook, for no amount of dole can keep up the morale, the spirit and the intellectual standard of those who have to spend their time in utter idleness (198)."

Isherwood The English novelist, Christopher Isherwood, was in Berlin and recreated this enforced idleness in his novels. In *Mr. Norris Changes Trains*, he wrote: "Morning after morning, all over the immense, damp, dreary town and the packing case colonies of huts in the suburb allotments, young men were waking up to another workless empty day to be spent as they could best contrive; selling boot-laces, begging, playing draughts in the hall of the Labour Exchange, hanging about urinals, opening the doors of cars, helping with crates in the market, gossiping, lounging, stealing, overhearing racing tips, sharing stumps of cigarette ends picked up in the gutter (199)."

By the end of 1931 over six million Germans were out of work, 72 and social conditions were grim indeed. An English Berlin

A demonstration of middle class unemployed in Berlin

correspondent spent an evening "in a certain red-lighted tavern ... Drinking my Pilsener and looking at a horse-meat sausage, I noticed that only at our table was anything being served. Round us sat comely young people ... I was told that everyone present was there to sell his or her body. We may wince at words, but what of the straits to which these children are driven by hunger?" The correspondent visited "a very poor family [where] the man had been unemployed for a year: his allowance had continued to diminish until now he was in receipt of thirty shillings a week for himself, his wife and nine children. They were living in two small rooms. Three cabbages for their daily meal of soup were simmering in a cauldron (200)."

The German middle classes suffered, too. Another visitor to Berlin reported hearing "innumerable stories of the misery of professional and business men and their families. Thousands who have inherited a cultivated standard of living now barely survive

German unemployment

73

on the charity of friends or on public funds. And they suffer now the uncertainty as to the immediate future: whether they will have enough to eat next month (201)."

Terror of inflation

Chancellor Bruning hoped desperately that the depression would pass of its own accord, and that war reparations would be cancelled, when Hoover's Moratorium ran out. Official German action was inhibited by terror of inflation. The German economist, Dr. M. J. Bonn, explained in the British press that, "for the moment, the fear of inflation and the will to avoid it at any price overshadows everything else in the public mind (202)." Everyone remembered the terrible collapse of the Deutschmark in 1924 and told stories of walls papered with worthless notes. They failed to grasp Keynes' idea that the slump could be fought by creating jobs through government spending. "Bruning spoke in the Sport Palace," wrote Isherwood. "His voice quivered with dry academic passion. 'Inflation!' he threatened, and the audience shuddered (203)."

Policy of deflation

Instead, Bruning fell back on a deflationary policy. He cut back business finance, economized on social services, reduced wages. Isherwood described how "each week there were new emergency decrees. Bruning's weary episcopal voice issued commands to the shopkeepers and was not obeyed (204)." Nor could the workers be persuaded to accept cuts. An English observer noted the "reduction of wages, since it is believed that the urgently necessary increase of turnover could then be achieved through lowering prices. Although the coal mines on the average are cutting out some five working shifts per month, the stocks on the dumps have increased [because] of the bad economic situation in Germany, and in the export trade. Sales for fuel to private homes are also very small at present, since a very large part of the population does not have money enough to purchase its winter supplies of coals . . . If one could promise the workmen that an increase in working shifts would result from lower wages and prices they would probably consent to a reduction in pay. But this is impossible (205)." Bruning's decrees won him the nickname of "the Hunger Chancellor;" he won little support.

Financiers blamed

The bitterness of those out of work, or badly paid, was fanned by the machinations of well-known international financiers. "Men

As the German mark plummetted in value, millions of pieces of worthless paper currency were printed. Armfuls of notes were needed for even the smallest everyday transaction

of the type of Ivar Kreuger moved rapidly from one capital city to another arranging without fuss or inconvenience to anybody what were described as 'good constructive loans' (206)." Sometimes these loans were neither good nor constructive. Not only were the financiers' vast private fortunes, made in the boom years, an insult to the starving; but during the depression their often unsound bonds collapsed, destroying personal savings. Financial fraud was common. The novelist Graham Greene wrote of his fictional speculator, that "honesty was a word which had never troubled him: a man was honest so long as his credit was good . . . A man of his credit did not go to prison. Kreuger, lying shot in the Paris hotel, was his example (207)." For when Kreuger's frauds were discovered, he killed himself.

Like every European paper, England's *Daily Express* gave such stories banner headlines, and reported that "drama, mystery and secrecy marked the end of the financial colossus who once directed the affairs of concerns with a stock market calculation of £160 millions (208)." The publicity given to such affairs accentuated the disgust with government. An English correspondent believed "that everyone in the land who is young and unemployed and hungry [feels] that his spirit is being stifled in the toils of big business, reparations and international finance (209)."

German bitterness   The Berlin correspondent of the *Chicago Daily News* told how enforced reparations worsened the effects of the depression: "The young chemist, engineer, teacher, lawyer, doctor [and] even the artisan, found the road blocked by his father and elder brother . . . The hatred of the disinherited swelled [against] a system that had accepted from the victorious Allies a treaty [that] meant the castration of Germanism. Without the Versailles Treaty these young men [would] have turned against the economic beneficiaries of the system and perhaps succeeded in eliminating them. As it was, with sixty per cent of each new university graduating class out of work, with over half of all Germans between the ages of sixteen and thirty unemployed, young Germany was an easy victim for the patriotic demagogue (210)." These were prophetic words.

Hitler   Adolf Hitler was one "patriotic demagogue" who realized that these resentments could be turned to personal advantage. Hitler was not unduly upset by the starved life of the unemployed. He actually wrote in the Nazi press: "Never in my life have I been so well disposed and inwardly contented as in these days. For hard reality has opened the eyes of millions of Germans (211)." Playing on German discontent, he promised in his election campaigns to end poverty, to "bring down the money barons," refuse reparation payments, and repudiate the humiliating Peace Treaty of Versailles of 1919.

Indeed, Dr. Bonn had already warned that "increased unemployment and bankruptcy are fertile seed beds for radical movements . . . National Socialism (Nazism) and Communism are not the outcome of prosperity but the fruit of prolonged depression and political humiliation (212)." Dr. Bonn was echoed by others: "That there are thirteen million Nazis and six million Communists is chiefly due to hunger (213)." The anger, as well as the numbers of these two extremist parties, grew apace. Whenever Nazis and Communists met in the streets, violence broke out. Christopher Isherwood described how "hate exploded suddenly, without warning, out of nowhere; at street corners, in restaurants, cinemas, dance halls, swimming baths . . . Knives were whipped out, blows were dealt with beer-mugs, chair legs, or leaded clubs; bullets slashed the advertisements on the poster columns, rebounded from the iron roofs of latrines (214)."

The slump had increased Communist strength; indeed, their influence helped Hitler's rise to power. Successive Chancellors were unable to form governments with workable majorities without Communist support. In order to save the Republic from collapse, President Hindenburg was forced to invite Hitler to become his Chancellor, in January, 1933. When Hindenburg died the following summer, "Hitler did what no one expected. He made himself both President and Chancellor . . . The man is resourceful," wrote an American journalist in his diary (215).

Hitler gains power

Nazi posters at the 1933 May Day celebrations proclaimed that "Adolf Hitler is your friend! Adolf Hitler is fighting for your freedom! Adolf Hitler will give you bread!" How would Hitler succeed where successive Chancellors had failed? An English correspondent saw the Germans "fed day by day on Hitler's oratory, dazzled with pictures of the glorious German past and promises of a still more glorious future . . . But enthusiasm cannot be indefinitely maintained on promises. It needs bread. The question is whether Adolf Hitler knows how to fulfil his promise to give Germany bread. It was expected that the May Day speech would contain a definite programme. But in fact we heard [nothing] that looks like solving the economic problem (216)."

This was Hitler's plan to solve the problem: "The Minister of Labour, Herr Seldte, has made public his programme for creating employment. It provides for giving work to 700,000 unemployed this year . . . The nucleus of the programme is the appropriation of one million marks in Treasury certificates for public works, [the] repair of houses [and] road building. The unemployed who are occupied in this way, will receive only the unemployment dole [and] 'certificates' of the value of twenty-five marks for each four weeks which can be used for buying clothing, linen or utensils for the house, but not for foodstuffs. The Reich issues these certificates at its own cost. In return the public institution that orders the work must furnish the worker one warm meal daily (217)."

Hitler's economic plans

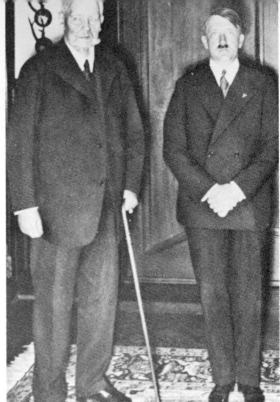

Left Adolph Hitler addresses a meeting; *right* Ex-Corporal Hitler with President von Hindenburg

Not only was this humiliating for the workers, but the public works schemes themselves were unambitious. Like Bruning, Hitler did not really believe it was possible to spend Germany out of the depression. Such schemes "are likely to cost a mint of money which in the present circumstances it may be difficult to find [and] they are likely to provide employment for a good many less people than the more innocent and optimistic of the Nazis may suppose (218)." Later that year, another commentator reported that "the Nazi government has not yet wrought any fundamental changes in German economic life. It has reorganized the political system; it has scarcely yet entered the economic field. The 'Leader' has probably no very clear cut views on economics apart from his emotional socialism . . . He has taken the advice of his business friends who helped to finance the movement (219)."

Hitler's rich allies

Hitler desperately needed money from the pockets of these "business friends" for his campaigns, his propaganda, his full-time officials and his private army. His press secretary, Otto Dietrich, wrote later that "in the summer of 1931 the Führer suddenly decided to concentrate systematically on cultivating the influential magnates (220)." An Englishman in Berlin at this time had warned his friend Lord Balfour that "Hitler plays more and more into the hands of his big industrial friends [who] will use him as a supporter of armaments." The industrialists had a vested interest in rearmament. Only a few months after the Nazis had gained power the *New York Herald Tribune* reported that "Adolf Hitler will proclaim Germany's demand for equality in armaments to the world in a set speech in the Reichstag (221)." At the same time, the Minister for Economic Affairs, speaking in Cologne, warned his audience that "emergency public works could not be more than a stimulus to employment . . . It was no use to pin faith to public works alone (222)."

Hitler pinned his faith to rearmament: it was at once the flower of his ambitions and his answer to the depression. The collapse of the World Disarmament Conference in 1933 (Chapter Seven) freed him from any inhibitions he might have had. In January, 1934, Kingsley Martin wrote that "every week munition workers in Germany let us know secretly what arms they are making, how their factories are working day and night (223)."

Germany rearms

From 1934 the German economy was geared to full-scale rearmament. As Hubert Henderson noted later in a Treasury memorandum, German "policy was to develop her strength for war . . . selective import control was the instrument upon which Germany mainly relied. She cut down ruthlessly her imports of commodities which her people could do without or could provide for themselves, and by this means she made more foreign exchange available for the materials she wanted for her war preparations . . . Starting from a position of decisive military inferiority in 1933 Germany had attained by 1938 the overmastering ascendancy which enabled Hitler to dictate the terms of Munich (224)."

The huge Hermann Goering steel works, the arms factories and the growth of related industries such as synthetic rubber and textiles, provided many jobs. Between February 1933 and the Spring of 1937 unemployment dropped from six millions to less than one million. "The people were, of course, aware that Hitler

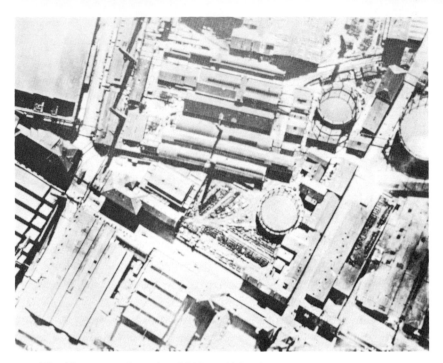

The Krupp steel works (1923), which played an important part in Germany's secret rearmament

was vigorously rearming Germany," said Otto Dietrich, "But he had provided millions with work and bread, had raised the standard throughout Germany. Why should the people distrust him? (225)."

Mussolini and Italy

The Great Depression gave Hitler power; Benito Mussolini's success had been achieved during the post-war slump. Oswald Mosley wrote that "the Italian disintegration, economic, political and psychological was extreme and brought Mussolini and the Fascists to power (226)." Mussolini had marched on Rome in 1922. Three years later he had declared in the Italian Chamber: "In front of the Italian people . . . I and I alone assume the political, moral and historic responsibility of everything that has happened. Italy wants peace and quiet, work and calm. I will give these things (227)." Unlike Hitler, who could present himself as the worker's saviour from poverty, Mussolini had already accepted full liability for their condition before the slump came. An English correspondent pointed out that, in the first few months of the depression, "Most countries have muddled along without policy,

"Il Duce:" the Italian dictator Benito Mussolini on a visit to Hitler in Berlin (1937)

without even a bad policy, much less a good one. But Mussolini cannot afford to fail. Herr Bruning and Ramsay MacDonald are, at is were, entitled to confess themselves beaten by circumstances; but Signor Mussolini is obliged to prove himself superior to circumstances (228)."

Before the darkest days of the depression, the Italian Socialist leader Francesco Nitti had sent Ramsay MacDonald a note on Italy's economic position; it was to be used in debate against Stanley Baldwin's defence of Italy's Fascist regime. Tourists in Italy "can see but little of the real situation, because of an outward appearance of order imposed by force . . . In spite of declarations to the contrary, the public debt has increased; in spite of lower real wages and salaries the Government has found it necessary to increase taxation . . . Industrial production is lagging behind, commerce is hampered, unemployment and bankruptcy are a menace to the nation's life . . . It is well known that the American loans to the cities of Milan and Rome, of thirty millions of dollars each, were used in the most lavish and extravagant

Italian economy

81

way . . . American investors must know that their new loans, if they succeed in prolonging for a little while the life of the Fascist regime, [will] not prevent the final collapse (229)."

Mussolini's Corporate state

In fact these American loans were withdrawn soon after the Wall Street crash later that year. Nitti claimed that Mussolini "has not only impoverished and discredited Italy, but is now preparing an appalling economic situation (230)." Mussolini may not have caused the economic crisis, but he certainly took advantage of the slump to tighten his grip on Italy through the so-called corporate state. Throughout industry, capital and the workers combined in companies under Government control. "It was evident from the beginning that the corporative system could not stop at the regulation of wages, hours of work and similar problems," wrote one observer when Mussolini set up the National Council of Corporations in 1929: "The Bill gives to the Council true legislative powers (231)." Il Duce was the president of each corporation and of the new Council.

"At first," the British Consul in Rome told Foreign Secretary Sir John Simon, "the relatively low standard of living, reductions in wages and longer hours of work prevailing here, enabled Italy to hold her own in many overseas markets (232)." In 1931, however, "Signor Mussolini finds himself perhaps for the first time in serious economic difficulties . . . officially the number of unemployed is in the neighbourhood of half a million; but there must be added much semi-employment . . . Obviously this means misery for a large proportion of Italian workers, and recently in the big towns of Northern Italy there has been raised the clamorous cry of 'Passports or bread!,' while the workless have paraded, with their pockets turned inside out (233)."

Next year the British Consul reported to London: "The number of unemployed . . . stands as I write at about 900,000 . . . As in every other country the rise in the number of unemployed has lowered the purchasing power of the community and so creates an ever widening vicious circle of increasing unemployment (234)."

Mussolini cuts 82 spending

Mussolini used his dictatorial powers to try and correct the situation. Like MacDonald in England and Bruning in Germany, Mussolini believed that depression demanded deflation. He "decreed a reduction of 12 per cent of the salaries of officials and of state employees. Then the shopkeepers were ordered to bring down their prices and the landlords to bring down their rents; transport, gas, electricity [were] reduced. It was hoped by this means to balance the budget, to diminish the costs of agriculture and to give Italian industry an advantage in international markets (235)." The "battle for wheat" produced a bumper crop in 1933 and made Italy independent of foreign cereals. Mussolini really did make the trains run on time. The railways were electrified and roads were built.

Public works relieved unemployment a little. The most spectacular of these was the reclamation of the Pontine Marshes. Sir Eric Drummond, British Ambassador in Rome, wrote to Sir John Simon in 1934 that "one of the great Fascist land reclamation schemes was carried a step further on 15th April when His Majesty the King of Italy formally opened the Commune of Sabaudia, the second to be reclaimed from the Pontine Marshes. Only 253 days passed between the date of the laying of the foundation stone of the new town and this week's ceremony. During this period there have never been less than two thousand hands at work on the town; at times as many as 4,500 have been engaged on it (236)."

The price for some measure of economic stability was high in terms of human freedom. But even critics of the regime were ready to acknowledge its efficiency. The British Consul wrote to Simon: "I spent a good deal of time with Dr. Borsa, [an] anti-fascist who has suffered for his creed to the extent of not being allowed to exercise his profession on an Italian newspaper. He spoke without bitterness of the shortcomings of the regime. He admitted its great achievements and summed up by saying, 'I would accept it all, every bit, but I want my liberty of speech' (237)."

Yet even Mussolini's wide Government intervention was not expansionist enough to stem the tide of the depression. In the Summer of 1933 an official at the English Embassy in Rome wrote to London that "revenue is dwindling and taxation already as high as can be borne. The upper class [is] living very largely on credit. The middle class [now] live their home life in a lack of comfort and on a diet [which is] considerably below the standard of the British artisan. The working classes are comparatively best off. A good deal is done for them by the government [and] they get the 'circuses' of organized excursions, reduced railway fares, cheap concerts and so forth (238)."

	Germany	Italy	France
November 1928	1,403,455	282,397	11,457
1929	1,760,653	–	11,917
1930	3,320,413	446,496	18,498
1931	4,722,801	799,744	122,824
1932	5,196,335	956,357	292,552
1933	3,775,934	962,868	286,874
1934	2,353,575	905,114	416,552
1935	1,984,925	*	453,838
1936	1,197,190	*	453,821
* Mussolini refused to publish figures for these years			

A table showing the numbers of unemployed in Germany, Italy, and France from November, 1928, to November, 1936

Italian finances were helped by reform of the banking system in 1934. In the same year, as all hope for the International Disarmament Conference faded, Mussolini began to rearm. In May, Rome's "Official Gazette reports an increase in the Italian naval estimates of £8,000,000 (239)." Later that month Mussolini told the Chamber of Deputies of his decision to build two 35,000-ton battleships. He "added that the Air Force would be renewed at the cost of another £11,000,000 ... The proposed programme would mean employment for all the different types of workmen and a sense of moral tranquillity for many Italian families (240)."

The corporate state was able to stamp out opposition by censorship and force. "Besides the army and the regular police, there are no less than six Fascist armed organizations with the sole purpose of preventing possible rebellions," wrote Francesco Nitti to Ramsay MacDonald in London (241).

South America

In South America, the dictators were less successful in managing the unemployed. "More and more Latin America seems to be feeling the economic pinch, and the political explosions in which

Mussolini speaking from the Roman Forum to Italian ex-servicemen

she expresses her 'malaise' go on spluttering like fireworks (242)."
In Chile, where 100,000 of the 140,000 miners lost their jobs,
Ibanez was forced to resign. Then in October, 1932, the same
correspondent reported that "in the once stable and sensible Chile
the past fortnight has seen another revolution come and go. The
provisional President Señor Davilar was deposed [by] the Com-
mander of the Air Force and the Director-General of the Navy
(243)." Uribura and Batista seized power in the Argentine and in
Cuba. There was much bloodshed and little order. Their military
dictatorships only worsened the depression in their countries.

Other would-be imitators of Mussolini came to Rome. A
Japanese professor just returned home to Tokyo said he was "sure
that the necessary conditions for a Fascist regime exist today in
Japan. We have the failure of the existing system; we have an
emergency which demands immediate action; we have the movement backed by the force of the army. One thing is lacking: a
Mussolini (244)."

Japan

Oswald Mosley, too, visited Mussolini in 1932 and was very

85

much impressed with him: "Our talks ranged widely over poli-tics . . . I like him, and found him easy to get on with (245)." Mosley returned home, turned his New Party into the British Union of Fascists, and began enlisting his blackshirts. His mass meetings in London and elsewhere caused violence. At Olympia in June, 1934, a journalist commented: "Sir Oswald Mosley had nothing of theatricalism to learn from either Hitler or Mussolini," and reported that "mounted police with drawn batons had to be called on to break up the struggling crowd (246)."

Happily, these scenes were only a pale shadow of the violence in Berlin. Mosley did not become a dictator; his movement failed. His own excuse for failure, an exaggeration of the facts, highlights the relationship between the depression and the rise of Fascism: "The circumstances we encountered in our British movement varied as widely from the experience of the German party as our policies differed from theirs. The German party was carried upwards on unemployment figures rising to a peak of catastrophe, which demanded a great change in government, while with an illusion of increasing prosperity, the rulers of Britain were saved from facing the results of their economic errors by external events (247)."

6 *The New Deal*

PRESIDENT Herbert Hoover's troubles had not ended with the Wall Street crash. Like their European cousins, the Americans had to find a way of handling the slump which followed. "When the first news of the New York Stock Exchange collapse . . . burst on the amazed American public it was freely prophesied that a hard winter was in store and that unemployment would be serious. Unemployment," the writer added, "has forced its way to the front pages of the newspapers, it is in fact too big a problem to be ignored any longer . . . The general estimate varies between about three and four millions [and] Philadelphia in March estimated the unemployed as over 50,000; Boston [counted] its unemployed in April as 41,466 out of a population of 402,394 adults (248)."

American unemployed

A visitor to New York described the "hardship, misery and degradation . . . Times Square is packed with shabby, utterly dumb and apathetic looking men. Nowhere in New York or any other city can one escape from the visible presence of those who are called 'the idle' (249)." The hero of a contemporary novel was one of "the idle." "The young man walks by himself through the crowd that thins into the night streets; feet are tired from hours of walking . . . muscles ache for the knowledge of jobs, for the roadmender's pick and shovel work . . . the engineer's slow grip wise on the throttle (250)." If he, or anyone else, felt like singing, the tune would probably have been the most popular song of the early thirties, "Brother, Can you Spare a Dime?"

Hardship

The novelist, Nathaniel West, set his novel *A Cool Million* against the same grim background in New York. "Times had grown exceedingly hard with the inhabitants of that once prosperous metropolis and Lem's ragged, emaciated appearance caused no adverse comment. He was able to submerge himself in the great army of unemployed." One day, when Lem visited the "Golden Gates Employment Bureau," his fortunes suddenly improved. "'My boy!' exclaimed Mr. Gates, the proprietor, 'We have obtained a position for you.' At this news, tears welled up in Lem's good eye and his throat was so choked with emotion that he could not speak."

Government silence This was the desperate atmosphere facing Hoover's Republican Government. Hoover later wrote: "With the Stock Market crash the primary question at once arose as to whether the President and the Federal Government should undertake to mitigate and remedy the evils stemming from it. No President before had ever believed there was a government responsibility in such cases (251)." Mellon, still Secretary of the Treasury, thought the slump would right itself like a ship in a storm. The slump would even "urge the rottenness out of the system. High costs of living and high living will come down. People will work harder [and] enterprising people will pick up the wrecks from less competent people (252)."

Hoover himself accepted the laissez-faire doctrine of the role of the government in the economy. A "rugged individualist," he continued to try to convince both himself and the people that the slump would soon be over and was in fact already declining. Frances Perkins—a social worker and later Roosevelt's Secretary of Labour—wrote that in the January after the crash "I read a story on the front page of the *New York Times* that President Herbert Hoover had told the press that there had been a gain in employment in the past week. He indicated that things were much better . . . I was horrified, for I knew that he had been greatly misinformed." She added, "I knew it was going to hurt the people being laid off in great numbers . . . I knew wives would read the story and reproach their husbands. I knew that young people would read the story and say 'Why doesn't Papa work?' (253)."

Roosevelt calls for action But Hoover went on merely hoping. The Democrat, Franklin D. Roosevelt, attacked him in an angry speech in Buffalo in the Autumn: "Although the times called for quick and decisive action by the Federal Government, nothing happened but words.

New York in the 1930s: *left* drab life on the Lower East Side; *right* an
angry meeting of the unemployed

This was the time if ever when Government projects should have
been accelerated [and] when public works should have been
pushed to provide employment (254)." Hoover was glad that his
pet scheme for river development would provide work: "We can
now build the many remaining segments of a definite canalization
of our river systems . . . it will provide employment for thousands
of men (255)." But he did not expect to set up relief schemes for
their own sake. Moreover, the budget had to be balanced. A
Republican senator described the "flood of unrelated and impossible
relief bills for hundreds of thousands of dollars more than the
yearly revenue of the government (256)," which were brought
before Congress; they had no chance of acceptance by Hoover
and Mellon.

Not only were Government relief schemes too expensive; they

would harm the moral integrity of the people. So "the basis of successful relief is to mobilize and organize the infinite number of agencies of self-help in the community. That has been the American way of relieving distress among our own people," wrote Hoover (257). But, as others pointed out in 1930, "Private charity, on which the workless must principally rely, is being severely strained and the leading charity organizations have had a hard time in their efforts to cope with the needy at their doors. On 18th March, 2,500 unemployed stood for hours in Pittsburgh in a 'bread line' waiting for a piece of bread and a bowl of soup, and this number was not unusually large. In New York the situation is very much worse, and as many as 12,000 meal tickets were distributed by the Bowery branch of the Y.M.C.A. on 17th March (258)."

By 1932 the strain on the agencies had increased with the numbers out of work. A correspondent wrote from Tennessee that "the American Federation of Labour has estimated that the 11 million unemployed receive only [an] average of two dollars a month to a family. There is a migratory class that falls outside the province of relief organizations. Perhaps a quarter of a million boys and young men drift from one side of the country to the other seeking work . . . Colonies of the unemployed who cannot obtain charity have grown up about the refuse dumps and garbage deserts in the large industrial centers (259)."

Hoover waits While the hungry queued, Hoover talked. A correspondent told his British readers that "cables from your side indicate that some mistrust is felt on account of [the] calling of so many conferences in Washington (260)." The President "summoned to the White House representatives from the railroads, the manufacturing interests, organized labour, agriculture, builders and financiers to confer on the economic state of the country (261)." He told the delegates: "We have asked you to confer together [on] the problems of the depression. The purpose is to better organize private initiative so as to further [the] progress of recovery of business, agriculture and employment [not] to pass resolutions on economic questions but to give you the opportunity to organize for action (262)." With such limited terms of reference these conferences achieved little and came to be known as "no-business meetings."

Like J. H. Thomas's negotiations with the British industrialists, they lacked any positive economic theory and workable sanctions.

Early 1932 brought a new low point of the American depression. *The worst* The National Bureau of Economic Research found that stocks had *days (1932)* fallen 83 per cent from the 1929 peak; production was down 40 per cent; wages were down 60 per cent; dividends were down 57 per cent. In his epic contemporary novel, *U.S.A.*, John dos Passos wrote: "That winter, the situation of the miners in the Pittsburgh district got worse and worse. Evictions began. Families with little children were living in tents and in broken-down unheated tar-paper barracks. Mary lived in a feeling of nightmare, writing letters, mimeographing appeals, making speeches at meetings for clothing and fur workers, canvassing wealthy liberals . . . She was thin and haggard and coughed all the time (263)." Millions of Americans had been thrown out of work.

Hoover cut the salaries of state officials, including his own by *Hoover's* 20 per cent. His deflationary policy allowed him to take some *deflation* steps: make small loans to farmers, vote meagre road-building funds, and set up a half-hearted Reconstruction Finance Corporation to lend money for industry. As Roosevelt said, "this has been unable to do more than put temporary patches on a leaking roof without any attempt to put a new roof on our economic structure (264)." Hoover hoped his actions in the international sphere—his tariffs and his Moratorium—would cure what, he convinced himself, was a European and not basically an American problem. His no-business meetings were designed to secure confidence: "business as usual." But people were not convinced. The *New York World* commented that "every time an administration official gives out an optimistic statement about business conditions the market immediately drops (265)," and an election placard in 1932 cried "In Hoover we trusted; now we are busted!"

Speaking at the Chicago election convention during the 1932 *New Deal* presidential campaign, Roosevelt told the American people: "I *pledge* pledge you, I pledge myself, to a new deal for the American people (266)." After the Democrats' victory, Roosevelt began working to restore the confidence in the Government forfeited by Hoover: "Let me assert my firm belief that the only thing we have to fear is fear itself . . . The money changers have fled from their high

The inauguration of President Franklin D. Roosevelt in 1937

seats in the temple of our civilization. We may now restore that temple to the ancient truths (267)." In the first of a series of broadcasts which came to be known as his "fireside chats," Roosevelt said: "Let us unite in banishing fear, [for] it is your problem no less than it is mine. Together we cannot fail (268)." One writer commented: "For the first time in half a generation the American people have elected a President who gives his fellow citizens the heartening picture of a joyous American working with zest and smiling as though he had no misgivings for the future of the United States (269)."

But "no President in American history has ever taken office in more trying circumstances than those that confront Mr. Roosevelt (270)." The main banks collapsed on the day of his inauguration. Fifteen million people had no work; the farmers were striking in an effort to force the government to guarantee a minimum price for their produce. "The farm strike in Iowa has gained dramatic prominence ... its significance lies in the fact that the conservative, land-owning farmers have gone on to the highways armed with clubs and pitchforks (271)."

It was not clear to contemporaries just how Roosevelt would
deal with the situation. H. V. Hodson, the economist, wrote that
"unemployment cried aloud for massive expenditures of public
money [and] as no one was prepared for higher taxation, large-
scale government borrowing was the only means of finance. The
President, however, was not by any means so convinced that
inflation must be preferred, among the instruments available to
him for the assault upon depression. He came to the White House
with an open mind upon monetary policy (272)."

Roosevelt kept his mind open and was always receptive to new
ideas. His lack of dogmatism was one of his strengths; the other
side of the coin was the lack of consistent theory behind his
policy. *Time* magazine later told the story how, "in the heat of the
Presidential campaign of 1936, the local Democratic headquarters
received a telephone call. 'Say!' a voice exclaimed, 'tell us just
what the principles of the New Deal are; we're having an argument!' 'Hold the phone,' was the answering injunction, followed
by a long pause. Then: 'Sorry, we're having an argument, too.'
(273)."

Roosevelt's acceptance of the need for state intervention was
clear, even if the methods he would use were a source of speculation. In his "New Deal" speech in July he had urged Americans
to "lay hold of the fact that economic laws are not made by
nature. They are made by human beings (274)." And in his
inaugural address of 4th March, 1933, he promised "action, and
action now," in this "dark hour of national life." He added, "We
do not distrust the future of essential democracy. The people of
the United States have not failed. In their need they have registered
a mandate that they want direct, vigorous action. They have asked
me for discipline, and direction under leadership. They have
made me the present instrument of their wishes. In the spirit of
the gift, I take it."

Roosevelt rapidly translated words into action. On 9th March
Congress was called, and in the famous Hundred Days (March to
July, 1933) passed thirteen vital measures. These won Roosevelt
praise as the rescuer of America from the horrors of the slump,
but also bitter accusations of dictatorship in private lives.

The Agricultural Adjustment Act of 12th May was designed

"to relieve the existing national economic emergency by increasing agricultural purchasing power (275)." It aimed to raise prices and provide cheap credit for farmers. How would the Act be financed? Roosevelt had not accepted the Keynesian idea of spending his way out of the slump. Raymond Moley, his Assistant Secretary of State, wrote later that "in his budget message, he made it plain that he was not committing himself to the policy of purposeless public spending and that he intended to bring the budget into balance as rapidly as possible (276)." Congress pushed Roosevelt into deflation by insisting that the Act should guarantee to farmers a price for their output no less than their costs of production.

On the other hand, Lionel Robbins criticized the Act for its failure to adopt an expansionist policy: "It proposes to restrict production by paying farmers to throw land out of cultivation . . . thus the net effect of the state intervention in American agriculture is this: the industrial workers will pay more for their food and the farmers continue to pay high prices for industrial products (277)."

The Act was also fiercely criticized for the extent of the powers granted to the Agricultural Adjustment Administration. An American journalist described in his diary a weekend with a friend on Long Island. "He was preoccupied with Franklin Roosevelt's 'dictatorship,' as he called it. He seemed deeply resentful that the New Deal would not allow him to grow potatoes in his garden (278)." But despite the lack of a consistent theory behind the Act, and even though it did nothing to help those who had been forced to give up their land during the slump, it did raise price levels through crop reduction and give the farmers the cheap credit they demanded.

Federal *Relief* Roosevelt, unlike Hoover, accepted full Government responsibility for all those out of work. He introduced a Federal Relief Emergency Act, "authorizing an appropriation of $500 millions for unemployment relief (279)," and he realized the need for public works as well as for the dole. "When President Roosevelt took office, [all] sorts of schemes were suggested by which to end the depression; and none did he receive more seriously than the proposal for expenditure on public works (280)." Roosevelt's scheme was introduced in the National Industrial Recovery ("Blue Eagle") Act of 16th June. The *New York Herald Tribune* carried the headlines, "Roosevelt Opens Recovery Drive; Five Million New Jobs his Goal," and reported his speech in Congress: "The law I have just signed was passed to put people back to work ... The Act gives employment by a vast programme of public works ... We should be able to hire many men at once and step up about a million new jobs by October, a much greater number later (281)."

All those who found work through the operation of the Act were regulated by a scheme of codes. These were designed to regulate hours of work, keep up production, and ban industrial practices which were against the national interest.

But the President's rigid belief in balancing the budget meant that N.I.R.A. schemes were not ambitious enough. A year later "the results thus far ... of the bold plan of 'made work' ... have proved disappointing. In spite of all the promises made there are at least ten millions unemployed and their number has recently shown a tendency to rise slightly (282)." The same year Dos Passos wrote an essay describing the "grim realities behind the rosy smoke screen of the New Deal ... Unemployment has come to stay, real wages are going down, America has few opportunities to offer young men growing up to take their places in the world (283)."

The other reason for the poor result of these public works was the opposition of businessmen. "It was felt that money should be spent only on things which did not compete with private industry— a fact which narrowed the field greatly ... Private employers complained that the Government operations were making it hard for them to obtain labour at the low prices they felt were necessary (284)." While Congress was pushing Roosevelt towards spending, powerful business tycoons were the "sound-money" men terrified of inflation. As well as fearing inflation they resented the enormous powers Roosevelt had taken for himself in his legislation. He was, after all, encroaching on their old spheres of influence. He had come to the White House, as Hodson said "with a convinced distrust of bankers, big business and money power generally (285)."

The battle between Roosevelt and big business was joined not only over the public works schemes, but over the main proposals

Business opposition

95

of the N.I.R.A. which brought federal control of the entire industrial structure. Roosevelt called this "the most important and far reaching legislation ever enacted by the American Congress . . . Its goal is the assurance of a reasonable profit to industry and living wages to labour (286)." The codes for employers and workers tried to establish a maximum hour week and a minimum wage rate. The President's right to intervene in the negotiations laid down by the codes for settling disputes was much resented by the industrialists. Hoover later recalled that he "tried to show that this stuff was mere fascism; that it was merely a remaking of Mussolini's 'corporate state' and refused to agree to any of it (287)." In 1935 the N.I.R.A. was invalidated by the Supreme Court as unconstitutional. The Presidential powers of intervention under the Agricultural Adjustment Act were also declared unconstitutional, and suffered the same fate. The money changers had not, after all, been driven out of the temple.

Roosevelt's own lieutenant, Moley, suggested that the President's hatred of the businessmen forced him into an egocentric position: "I began to wonder whether Roosevelt had begun to see his program as an end in itself, rather than as a means to an end; whether he wasn't beginning to feel that the proof of a measure's merit was the extent to which it offended the business community (288)." During his second term of office, the battle involved Roosevelt in an unfortunate attempt to put his own supporters in the Supreme Court, to save the rest of his New Deal. His enemies took full advantage of this, by raising their cries of "Fascist!" and "Dictator!"

The rise in agricultural prices achieved by the A.A.A. and the agreements on working conditions secured by the N.I.R.A. had done something, before these Acts were invalidated, to help farmers and workers towards recovery. The other legislation of the Hundred Days concentrated on reform. The Securities Exchange Act of 27th May regulated the Stock Exchange to protect the public against devious stock manipulators and to prevent another great crash. The Emergency Banking Act established Governmental control over the banks. It allowed the Federal Reserve Bank to issue more money, and so loosen credit. The United States now went off the gold standard, and banned the export of gold and

Monetary reforms

Opposite above Franklin D. Roosevelt giving one of his famous "fireside chats" on the radio; *opposite below* the Roosevelt Dam on the Salt River, part of the New Deal programme of public works silver, and reduced the gold content of the dollar. Bank deposits were guaranteed through an insurance scheme. The significance of devaluation was understood by a visiting Frenchman, who wrote that "no matter how uncertain the future seems to be, one point has been established: the United States took the measure of directing the dollar. It is the Government that has taken hold of the wheel of the monetary command. In America now the state is master of its money (289)."

Tennessee Valley Authority

Roosevelt extended Government control to the waterways and their hydro-electric schemes as well as to industry, relief, banking and the Stock Market. The Tennessee Valley Authority Act (May, 1933) was designed "to improve the navigability and to provide for the flood control of the Tennessee River, to provide for the reforestation and the proper use of marginal lands in the Tennessee Valley (290)." It prevented the exploitation of these lands by private corporations. The success of this experiment led to a demand for the construction of other power sites and for regional planning by the Federal Government.

End of prohibition

At the end of all this exhausting legislation President Roosevelt relaxed. He declared, "I think this would be a good time for beer!" and ended prohibition. One newspaper pointed out that "it has even been estimated that [this] measure will create, directly and indirectly, a million jobs. While this estimate is obviously exaggerated, it is confidently believed that repeal of the Eighteenth Amendment will prove a powerful solvent to unemployment (291)."

Confidence revived

However successful or long lasting the laws of the Hundred Days may have been, they had at least restored confidence. Not only had something been done to fight the slump that Hoover had left to take its own course; action had been taken dramatically, and had been seen to be done. Roosevelt's fireside chats and his numerous public appearances made Americans identify with him. No less than half a million Americans had written to Roosevelt during the first week of the administration, to thank him for reviving hopes. In May, Walter Lipmann wrote: "The nation which had lost confidence in everything and everybody has regained confidence in the Government and in itself (292)." These sentiments were echoed elsewhere: "The defeatist or fatalistic atti-

Unemployed Americans queuing up for free meals at a soup kitchen

tude towards unemployment and the depression generally is much less common in the country than it was. It is utterly alien to the administration (293)."

Roosevelt's euphoric and contagious gaiety projected a romantic image of St. George slaying the dragon of the depression with the sword of the New Deal. This view was as exaggerated as that of the relentless dictator drawn by his enemies. Roosevelt defended himself against these attacks in one of his fireside chats: "Plausible self-seekers and theoretical diehards will tell you of the loss of individual liberty. Answer this question out of the facts of your life. Have you lost any of your rights, or liberty, or constitutional freedom of action of choice? (294)."

On the contrary, by swift action and a measure of economic management, Roosevelt had done much to bring "freedom from fear" and poverty. America owed him a healthier banking system and a revival of agriculture. Unemployment fell by five millions

Better Days

An unemployed American worker earning a few nickels by selling apples

between 1933 and 1937, even though until 1940 the national figure remained at least 10 per cent. The increased purchasing power of the farmers and the re-employed encouraged industry, despite the failure of the businessmen, in their antagonism to the New Deal policies, to make large-scale investment. Moley wrote that "by December, 1934, there was evidence that business was executing a slow and majestic upturn (295)."

Roosevelt's Hundred Days not only gave the American people confidence in themselves and in their President; they renewed confidence in the democratic system itself. One of Roosevelt's achievements was to counter extremist politics which could so easily have flourished in America as elsewhere. Unemployment was as serious as in Germany, but extremists never posed a real danger in America. By 1931 the Communists had gained surprisingly little support. A foreign correspondent remarked that "the great masses who subsist on meagre rations . . . give few indications of disaffection. The surface signs of a trend toward radical political philosophies are almost non-existent. Nor is there any apparent tendency toward violent revolt (296)." With the leap in unemployment from three to fifteen millions by 1933 there was more cause for alarm. Precautions were taken against riots in the large cities. They were never needed. Communist strikes in California, and among agricultural workers, all came to nothing.

Extremists forestalled

The fear of Communism gave way to the fear of Fascism. Only a month before Roosevelt's inauguration in March, 1933, Adolf Hitler had become the German Chancellor. The examples of authoritarianism in Germany and Italy were used by Hoover and others to discredit Roosevelt's Government. Others who had no suspicions of Roosevelt's own motives were also frightened. O. G. Villard wrote: "It is amazing how many there are who believe that our boasted democratic institutions will not survive the effect of two more years of our depression." A prominent figure assured him that "if President Roosevelt failed there would be a coalition government, to be followed in short order by a pure Fascist administration of the country (297)." Senator Huey Long hoped to take advantage of a popular demand for a strong man. But the New Deal revived faith in the existing two-party system and denied both Fascism and Communism the chance offered by the slump. Sir Isaiah Berlin believed that Mr. Roosevelt's greatest service to mankind was "that he showed that the fierce left and right wing propaganda of the thirties, according to which the conquest and retention of political power [needs] the systematic practice of despotism . . . was simply untrue. Mr. Roosevelt's example strengthened democracy everywhere (298)." Villard added that "if Mr. Roosevelt succeeds, the rest of the embattled world will

Roosevelt accused as dictator

be compelled to follow and adopt the American programme (299)."

Throughout the difficult years of America's depression, Roosevelt had acted pragmatically. He was no doctrinaire. The New Deal drew on every political and economic experience of the previous fifty years. It was neither totalitarian, as some extremists claimed; nor was it the "Red New Deal with a Soviet seal," as the Chicago *Tribune* claimed. In Roosevelt's own words, "We seek to guarantee the survival of private enterprise by guaranteeing conditions under which it can work."

Aftermath
In a sense, the New Deal worked too well. During the 1930s the trend toward monopoly grew, as so many smaller firms had collapsed during the depression. After five years of the New Deal, three firms produced four of every five American automobiles; three companies made 60 per cent of the steel; and one company virtually produced all American aluminium.

But by the Social Security Act (1934) with its range of social benefits, and the Wagner Act (1935), to safeguard "the practice and procedure of collective bargaining," President Roosevelt had done much to protect those millions whose livelihoods increasingly depended on the monolithic corporations. Roosevelt had largely fulfilled his aim "to remake national life after a fashion which, whether the old prosperity returned or not, would yield a larger sense of social justice, and meet the demands of a new democracy."

Swedish "New Deal"
The Swedish experiment in Economic Management began quite independently of the New Deal; but was encouraged by the example of President Roosevelt's Hundred Days. Its impetus came similarly from the slump. The British Ambassador in Stockholm wrote to London in 1931: "Sweden is suffering from the general economic depression, though in a lesser degree than most countries ... Her iron ore and timber interests have been especially hard hit ... Some authorities are apprehensive as to the magnitude of M. Kreuger's operations (300)." The workers went on strike in protest at their low pay and the unemployed were vociferous in their demands for jobs. In May, demonstrators in Adalen were killed when the police opened fire.

When Kreuger's financial empire folded the following year,

PRESIDENT'S REPORT (COMMITTEE ON UNEMPLOYMENT)		PERCENTAGE UNEMPLOYMENT	
Aug 1929	0.65 *millions*	Nov 1930	21%
Jan 1930	4.07	1931	26%
Jan 1931	8.05	1932	32%
Jan 1932	11.46	1933	27%
Mar 1933	15·07	1934	24%
Jan 1933	14.49	1935	20%
Jan 1934	12.60	1936	12%
Jan 1935	12.60		
Oct 1935	12.56		
Jan 1936			

The American unemployed (1930–36)

"the swiftest and most dramatic reaction was in Sweden, M. Kreuger's home country. A special session of Parliament was hastily summoned and the Government introduced a Bill designed to prevent the tragedy causing a panic. It provided for moratoria in case of need (301)." The collapse put many out of work, swelling the numbers of the hungry demonstrators.

The Government's answer to the situation, like the answers of Snowden, Bruning and Hoover, was deflation. A Stockholm correspondent reported that "although the Government is in nearly every case refusing requests for grants, and although the strictest economy is already being observed, the Government states that 'very considerable increases in taxation must be made in order to render possible the balancing of the budget.' The need for this step is understood to have been precipitated by the Kreuger crash (302)." In August, 1932, a British official reported that an official statement "shows the effects of the international trade depression on the finances of the country. Receipts were about nine million kroner less than the figure entered in the budget for the previous years (303)."

Swedish deflation

Falling trade and rising discontent swept the Swedish Social Democrats into power at the September, 1932, elections. Led by Per Albin Hansson, they pre-empted the Fascist threat with measures to outlaw private armies. Swedish democratic traditions helped to curb the Nazi movement's influence, and fostered support for the new Government's economic policies. The

Toward economic planning

reactionary National Union of Farmers, for example, agreed that men engaged in public schemes should receive a full working wage. A British Embassy official sent Anthony Eden a summary of Swedish Government policies: "The chief items are an extensive scheme of public works for the relief of unemployment and state aid for agriculture and forestry. The Government have also put through a scheme for voluntarily state aided unemployment insurance ... The whole programme for overcoming the crisis bears an interesting resemblance to that of President Roosevelt in the U.S.A., though it has not been pushed to such extremes (304)." Sweden's managed economy was both less extreme than America's, and more soundly backed by consistent theory. It was to become a blue-print for all democratic planners.

7 Keynes: Planning for Wealth

KINGSLEY MARTIN once said that "in the days when politics were politics, elections used to be rather fun. People could enjoy getting angry about Home Rule or the House of Lords. But now that politics are economics, elections are sheer bewilderment (305)." G. D. H. Cole, the economist, thought the public should be educated: "I believe that the understanding of present-day economic problems is not really so hard a matter as it is often made out to be ... The general election of 1931 turned largely on such economic issues as the balance of trade, the dangers of inflation, the effects of going off the gold standard, and the case for and against tariffs ... In every country the world slump has forced these questions into the forefront of political controversy (306)."

But even those who understood such technical phrases were muddled by the current economic debate. One of MacDonald's supporters found that "quite a lot of people are highly sceptical, in view of the extraordinary differences of opinion among the economists, as to whether there is in fact a sufficient body of precise knowledge to justify the firm claims of either side (307)." Much the same could be said of subjects like the European Common Market today.

But in the 1930s the rulers were almost as mystified as the ruled. Hoover wrote sadly that "as a matter of fact there was little economic knowledge to guide us (308)." Roosevelt disappointed Keynes when they met in 1934 because, as the economist told the President's Secretary of Labour, he "had supposed the President was more literate, economically speaking (309)." Hitler was criticized for having "no very clear-cut views on economics." Ramsay MacDonald showed his ignorance of Keynesian expansionist theories when he wrote to a friend: "This lean kine period has struck us just at a time when we ought to be spending large sums of money . . . and yet if we do that we are to create conditions which will add still further to unemployment. We are in a vicious swing (310)."

Leaders too cautious

Every Government was hampered in fighting the depression by their cautious financial orthodoxy. It was widely believed that the slump would right itself, and do so quickly; Government intervention was unnecessary. Even if the idea of economic control was accepted, it was inhibited by belief of the need for balanced budgets. As Oswald Mosley wrote, "The orthodoxy of the period utterly rejected . . . policies with a background of Keynesian economics (311)." Mosley himself accepted the significance of the new economics. He told British Members of Parliament that the country needed "a policy of manhood which takes the nation out into the field and builds up its muscles . . . It is a policy of planning which can only be entrusted to executive government (312)." His administrative and economic proposals could have begun a sophisticated experiment in planning. Lloyd George's 1929 election manifesto was also based on the need for government control of the economy; indeed, it closely resembled the New Deal of which he later so much approved. The British Cabinet Secretary wrote to an American friend that "Lloyd George has declared himself as much impressed by the enterprise of your President (313)."

Democracy in crisis

But Lloyd George and Mosley were rejected. The National Government arrived at a tentative policy of economic management in slow and pragmatic steps. Roosevelt, the Swedish socialists, and France more slowly, reached the same solution. Where democracy was less well entrenched as in the Weimar Republic of Germany, or where it had already yielded to Fascism as in Italy, the dictatorships imposed their own brand of management. Joseph Stalin had imposed his Five Year Plan on Russia in 1928: it had caused great hardship, increasing, not mitigating, the effects of the trade depression. "The authoritarian state systems of today," wrote Keynes, "seem to solve the problem of unemployment at the expense of efficiency and freedom . . . But it may be possible by a right analysis of the problem to cure the disease while preserving efficiency and freedom (314)."

The move towards Government economic planning followed the failure of deflationist policies. As Hubert Henderson later pointed out in a Treasury memorandum, "There was no surer prescription for the defeat of Governments during the inter-war period than persistence in deflation . . . The Bruning government set themselves to restore equilibrium by deflating costs and prices, and persisted in this course until the strains it caused swept away the republican regime and brought Hitler to power . . . A similar deflationary policy was to prove largely instrumental three years later in bringing M. Blum into office in France (315)." Successive French governments under Herriot, Daladier and others fell in the meantime in their efforts to provide jobs while balancing the budget. In the same way, Chamberlain's policies superseded Thomas's; Roosevelt followed Hoover; and the socialists came to power in Sweden. Professor Lionel Robbins wrote in 1934: "We may not all be socialists now, but we are certainly nearly all planners (316)." *Deflation useless*

While the depression encouraged Governments to plan at home, it pushed them into isolationism in their foreign policies. Henderson, then Secretary of the British Economic Advisory Council, told the Cabinet that "a period of falling world prices is a period of rising world tariffs. When trade is depressed and unemployment widespread, protectionist arguments gain greatly in their appeal . . . Public sympathy is aroused for the work people who have lost their employment, and the feeling grows that it is unwise national economy to allow imported goods to enter which might be made at home (317)." After the German bank collapse the Berlin correspondent of *The Economist* wrote: "The Government seems to be pushed further and further into protectionism." *Tariffs divide the world*

The following year President Hoover brought in the Hawley–Smoot tariffs. Senator Reed Smoot wanted "a high degree of self sufficiency" for the United States. Congressman Willis C. Hawley wished to make her "self-contained and self-containing (318)." Considering the fairly small part foreign trade played in the American economy, these tariffs seemed needlessly isolationist.

In Roosevelt's view they "drained the world of gold, made it impossible for foreigners to pay their debts and started trade reprisals over the world (319)." He was proved right. Chamberlain introduced British import duties in 1932, described in *The Times* as "based on retaliation . . . following the foolish train of international events which we set in motion when the Hoover law was enacted in 1930 (320)." Later, the main feature of Hitler's economic policy was to be a system of selective import controls.

War debts too heavy As Roosevelt had pointed out, rising tariffs made war debts an even heavier burden to shoulder. Resentment over the debts heightened international tension, and the move toward isolationism. Ramsay MacDonald received a letter from an American friend who had visited him in the Summer of 1931: "Since returning home I have been rather surprised to see how much antagonism exists to any thought of cancelling the war debts. I suppose it is in part due to the depths of depression which exists in the minds of most everybody here regarding our economic outlook. Indeed, it seems extremely difficult to get anyone here to look at our economic problem in relation to world problems (321)."

The British were just as resentful. Even before the introduction of the Young Plan the *Daily Telegraph* had written that "it must be remembered that Great Britain receives only 22 per cent of the total paid by Germany in reparation for war damage, and that if the German annual payment were scaled down our share would cease to be adequate to meet our payments to America (322)." Soon after the National Government took office, Steven Runciman pointed out how the system of reparations in kind made German payments fall far short of those demanded by America: "The payments which had to be made to this country from our late enemy could only be made in goods or services, or in kind . . . There was no gold available. We had the onus placed upon us of trying to transfer the credit in one form or another to America. Our goods were not acceptable; our services to a large extent were rejected. We handed over to America vast sums of gold (323)."

Hoover's Moratorium Hoover's Moratorium was welcomed as "a sign that the United States is coming out of its isolation from European affairs and that presently there may be a change of policy in Washington

(324)." The same journalist reported France's reaction to the Moratorium. Having a primarily agricultural economy, the French were only just feeling the pain of the depression: "The journalists of Paris have looked the gift horse in the mouth and found a very rotten set of teeth . . . The French politicians complain that Mr. Hoover, in being kind to Germany, is being too kind at the expense of France. The unconditional payments by Germany to France under the Young Plan make up some 5 per cent of the French budget. France says she cannot sacrifice such a large item (325)."

Americans feared that France and Britain might refuse to pay their debts when the Moratorium ran out. Villard wrote to Mac-Donald: "If you are compelled to cease paying it will create a tremendous outcry in the United States where people do not forget that monies we loaned England were the only things that just then kept England in the war . . . A failure on the part of England to pay, however defensible and just, will unquestionably increase tension between the two countries (326)."

At the Lausanne Conference in July, 1932, the powers, in Mac- *War debts* Donald's words "brought down the curtain on the long tragedy *unpaid* of reparations which has proved an economic curse alike on those who paid and to those who received them (327)." In British and French minds reparations and debts were indissolubly linked. Henderson believed that "if reparations go into the melting-pot, so assuredly will inter-Allied debts; and a most ugly international situation may easily ensue, which might entail unexpected repercussions in other parts of the world, and which would certainly destroy all hopes of successful international co-operation for such purposes as concerted reductions of tariffs and economy in the use of gold (328)." France and Britain both applied to the the United States for cancellation of their debts and, when it was refused, defaulted. This tearing up of a major international agreement naturally increased the tendency toward isolationism.

As Henderson predicted, the American reaction came at the World Economic Conference the following year. The day before the Conference opened, the *New York Times* wrote: "There are said to be at least thirty million unemployed workers throughout the world whose hope for re-employment must rest largely upon

The economist, John Maynard Keynes (1883–1936)

what this conference of nations can agree upon (329)." But Roosevelt disappointed these hopes. He placed his own country before his "good neighbour" policy by refusing to lower tariffs or stabilize currencies by signing any world monetary agreement. He told the Conference: "The sound economic system of a nation is a greater factor in its wellbeing than the price of its currency in changing terms of the currencies of other nations (330)."

A British official in Rome told the British Foreign Secretary that Roosevelt's decision "placed Italy in a position which may prove to be less and less tenable as time goes on (331)." Later in the year, at a Buckingham Palace garden party King George V told a visiting American that he and MacDonald had been made fools of at the Conference (332). This was the general European reaction. Keynes, however, understood, and agreed with Roosevelt's action: "The policy of national self-sufficiency, although not an ideal in itself or in the long run, is needed for the immediate future to guarantee each country its freedom while attempting to find a new mode of political economy. Let goods be homespun whenever it is reasonably possible and above all let finance be primarily national (333)." Keynes believed, like Mosley, that each country had to insulate itself from the outside world and nurture its own prosperity before signing international agreements. Professor Robbins, a more orthodox economist, attacked Keynes as he had previously attacked his tariff proposals: "What a pity that he should now turn his magnificent gifts to the service of the mean and petty devices of economic nationalism (334)."

Economic nationalism was now bound to follow in the wake of the World Economic Conference. Each country levied its own import restrictions; each country manipulated its own currency. Trade suffered because no-one knew which country would impose a tariff next, or devalue its currency. As one country gained a temporary advantage by devaluation others were forced to do the same. Just as Chamberlain's tariffs followed Hoover's so America followed Britain off the gold standard in 1933 and Leon Blum and the Popular Front were forced to do the same for France three years later. The year 1933 marked the watershed between the years of post-1919 idealistic internationalism, and the years of economic nationalism leading to 1939. In 1933 thirty

Economic nationalism

111

million people were out of work; the hope of ending the depression by international agreement ended. In Germany Hitler came to power.

An American journalist in Europe wrote in his diary: "The year just past, 1933, may very well have been one not only of transition for us personally but for all Europe and America. What Roosevelt is doing at home seems to smack almost of social and economic revolution. Hitler and the Nazis have lasted out a whole year in Germany (335)." The depression had brought both isolationism and Fascism. The collapse of the World Economic Conference had sabotaged the Disarmament Conference. Free from international controls, the German Nazis began to rearm for their own expansionist ends.

World War Two

Ironically, rearmament and war brought both employment and an acceptance of Keynesian economics. The Second World War (1939–45) forced governments to plan far more than ever they did in peace time. As the war drew to a close, governments realized the need to find a way of continuing such planning without damaging each other. Keynes was now at the British Treasury and a major influence on his Government's economic thinking. Although Keynes had advocated economic nationalism as a stop gap, he realized that open competition in import controls and currency adjustments had had a damaging effect on world trade.

Bretton Woods Conference

All this must now give way to international agreement. With Roosevelt's Treasury Secretary, Keynes arranged the Bretton Woods Conference in 1944. The powers met and listened to him. Professor Robbins, his old opponent, was as impressed as all the other delegates. He wrote in his journal: "Keynes was in his most lucid and persuasive mood; and the effect was irresistible. At such moments I often find myself thinking that Keynes was one of the most remarkable men that have ever lived—the quick logic, the birdlike swoop of intuition, the vivid fancy, the wide vision, above all the incomparable sense of the fitness of words, all combine to make something several degrees beyond the limit of ordinary human achievement ... The Americans sat entranced as the God-like visitor sang and the golden light played around. When it was all over there was very little discussion ... But I am clear that we are off with a flying start (336)."

The Bretton Woods Conference set up the International Monetary Fund (I.M.F.). This was designed "to promote international monetary co-operation and collaboration . . . To facilitate the expansion and balanced growth of international trade and to contribute thereby to the promotion and maintenance of high levels of employment . . . To promote exchange stability [and] to avoid competitive exchange depreciation . . . To give confidence to members by making the Fund's resources available to them under adequate safeguards, thus providing them with opportunity to correct maladjustments in their balance of payments without resorting to measures destructive of national or international prosperity (337)." Never again would the world witness another wild boom, Wall Street crash or economic blizzard. Governments would take firm control of their economies instead of falling victim to them.

International Monetary Fund

Economic management, or planning, became accepted in the domestic as well as the international field. This was the "right analysis" advocated by Keynes, denied by the followers of the "classical economists," and foreshadowed in varying degrees by Roosevelt, Chamberlain and the Swedish socialists. The debate on employment policy in the British House of Commons in 1944, no less than at the Bretton Woods Conference, was proof of Keynes' belief that "practical men, who believe themselves to be quite exempt from any intellectual influences are usually the slaves of some defunct economist . . . I am sure that the power of vested interests is vastly exaggerated compared with the gradual encroachment of ideas (338)." John Maynard Keynes' ideas had certainly impressed Ernest Bevin, British Minister of Labour: "In future," he said, "the Government's policy will be to meet the onset of any depression at an early stage by expanding and not contracting capital expenditure, and by raising consumption expenditure and not reducing it (339)."

Planning accepted

The idea of government intervention in economic matters was even more important than the method. It endowed a higher standard of living upon more people, all over the world, than ever before. Bevin declared: "we are turning our back, finally, on past doctrines and past conceptions and looking forward with hope to a new era (340)."

A new era

113

Further Reading

THE MOST important book for the understanding of the economic background of the period is John Maynard Keynes, *The General Theory of Employment Investment and Money*. These books on Keynes himself are particularly helpful: Donald Winch, *Economics and Policy*, and Roy Harrod, *The Life of John Maynard Keynes*. *Slump and Recovery* by H. V. Hodson is straightforward and informative; Lionel Robbins, *The Great Depression*, is a laissez-faire interpretation and should be read in conjunction with Hubert Henderson's more enlightened *The Inter-War Years and other Papers*.

J. K. Galbraith's account of *The Great Crash* not only manages to explain clearly the intricacies of the American stock market but is also very exciting. The best works on the period for the different national backgrounds are Arthur Schlesinger, *The Age of Roosevelt*; William Shirer, *The Rise and Fall of the Third Reich*; Alan Bullock, *Hitler*; Christopher Hibbert, *Mussolini*; Denis Brogan, *The Devlopment of Modern France 1870–1939*; and William Shirer, *The Collapse of the Third Republic*. For the English background the best works are A. J. P. Taylor, *English History 1914–45*, volume XV of The Oxford History of England, David Thomson, *England in the Twentieth Century* in the Pelican History of England, Francis Wilkins, *Family Life from 1930 to the 1980s* (Batsford, 1985), Michael Gibson, *Spotlight on the Interwar Years* (Wayland, 1986) and Nathaniel Harris, *The Great Depression* (Batsford, 1987). Robert Skidelski's *Politicians and the Slump* is a brilliant if over didactic study of the 1929–31 Labour Government; *1931 Political Crisis* is a detailed account by R. Bassett, a Labour candidate and MacDonald supporter at the time. Philip Snowden's *Autobiography* and *George Lansbury* by his son-in-law, Raymond Postgate, are both understandably biased, but entertaining.

The most vivid accounts of the social effects of the depression can be found in contemporary novels. Christopher Isherwood's *Mr. Norris Changes Trains* and *Goodbye to Berlin*; George Orwell's *Down and out in Paris and London*, *The Road to Wigan Pier* and *England, Your England*; John Dos Passos' *U.S.A.* all give graphic descriptions of life during the Great Depression.

Glossary

ANNUITY A fixed sum payable at specified intervals in return for a premium, paid either in instalments or as a single payment.

ANOMALIES Deviations from the normal or usual order; irregularities.

ARMAMENTS The weapons of a military ship, aircraft or vehicle.

BULL MARKET A market where speculators buy stocks in anticipation of rising prices, in order to make profit on resale.

CAPITAL GOODS Goods used in the production of other goods rather than being sold to consumers.

CAPITALISM The economic system based on private ownership of the means of production, distribution and exchange; capitalists operate and manage their property for profit in competitive conditions.

COALITION When groups combine into one body.

COMMUNIST A member of the movement which supports a classless society, where private ownership has been abolished.

DEBACLE A sudden, disastrous collapse.

DEVALUATION A decrease in the exchange value of a currency against gold or other currencies brought about by a government.

DISSEMINATE To distribute or scatter about.

DOVETAILING A contrived way of making things fit together neatly; for example making a question fit an answer.

EQUILIBRIUM A stable condition where outside influences are balanced.

EXPANSIONISM The practice of expanding the economy of a country.

FASCIST A follower of the political movement, Fascism, which encouraged militarism and nationalism.

FEDERAL CONTROL Controlled by government.

FLOTATION Launching or financing a business company by issuing shares which the public may buy.

INAUGURATION   To formally and ceremonially place in office.

INDICTMENT   A formal accusation of crime.

INFLATIONARY   Causing an increase in the general level of prices by an expansion in demand or money supply.

KINE   Cattle.

LAG   To fall behind.

LIQUIDATION   Terminating a business by selling its assets to pay its debts.

MERGER   Combining two or more companies either by creating a new organization or by one company absorbing the other.

MITIGATE   To make less severe.

MONOPOLY   An exclusive control of the supply of a product or service.

MORATORIUM   A legally authorized postponement of repayment of a debt.

PERTURBATIONS   Disturbances or upsets.

PROTECTIONISM   When duties are imposed on imports in order to protect domestic industries against overseas competition.

RATIONALIZATION   Justification of one's actions.

REICHSTAG   The building in Berlin, destroyed in 1933, where the officers of the Weimar Republic met.

REPARATION   The act of making amends.

REPUBLICAN   A supporter of the form of government where the people, or their elected representatives, have power.

REPUDIATE   Refuse to accept the validity of something.

SANCTION   Authorize or encourage.

SECURITIES   Financial assets, such as shares, which provide the owner with interest.

SPECULATION   Buying and selling securities in the hope of making money; investment involving high risk but also the possibility of high profit.

STOCK MARKET   The place where securities are regularly traded.

STOCK TICKER   The paper ribbon on which a tape machine at the stock market automatically prints current share prices.

Table of Events

1929

March 4th	Herbert Hoover becomes American President
March 4th	Bruning becomes Chancellor of Germany
May 30th	Second Labour Government takes office in Britain
August 27th	Hague Conference adopts Young Plan for reparations
October 24th	Wall Street crash (Black Thursday)
December 2nd	Benito Mussolini strengthens "Corporate State" in Italy

1930

January 23rd	Oswald Mosley's memorandum
May 20th	Mosley resigns from British Cabinet
June 13th	Hoover's Hawley-Smoot tariffs

1931

March 1st	Mosley forms his New Party
May 31st	Austrian Kreditanstalt Bank fails
June 20th	Hoover puts Moratorium on War Debts
July 13th	German banks collapse
July 31st	May Committee recommends British deflation
August 25th	National Government formed in Britain
September 21st	Britain abandons gold standard
September 28th	Ramsay MacDonald expelled from Labour Party

October 27th	National Government wins British election

1932

February 2nd	World Disarmament Conference
February 4th	Chamberlain's Imports Duty Bill
March 13th	Kreuger financial crash
May 8th	Herriot forms Radical Government in France
July 13th	Lausanne Conference ends war reparations
July 31st	Nazis win more than a third of votes in German election
September 24th	Swedish Social Democrats take office under Per Albin Hansson
November 6th	Franklin D. Roosevelt elected American President

1933

January 30th	Adolf Hitler becomes German Chancellor
March 4th	Roosevelt inaugurated as American President
March 9th	Roosevelt's Hundred Days of the New Deal begin
April 19th	United States abandons gold standard
May 12th	Agricultural Adjustment Act passed in U.S.A.
May 18th	Tennessee Valley Authority created
June 12th	World Economic Conference
June 16th	National Industrial Recovery Act passed in U.S.A.

1936

June 4th	Leon Blum forms Popular Front Government in France
September 28th	France abandons gold standard
October 5th	Jarrow march in England

1944

July 1st	Bretton Woods Conference sets up International Monetary Fund

Notes on Sources

(1) Presidential Campaign speech (11th August, 1928)

(2) Message to Congress (4th December, 1928)

(3) Herbert Hoover, *Memoirs*

(4) Oswald Mosley, *My Life*

(5) *The Economist* (10th December, 1927)

(6) *The Economist* (5th February, 1927)

(7) *New York Herald Tribune* (29th October, 1929)

(8) Frederick Lewis Allen, *Only Yesterday*

(9) Oswald Mosley, *My Life*

(10) Frederick Lewis Allen, *Only Yesterday*

(11) *Ibid*

(12) Quoted in Frederick Lewis Allen, *Only Yesterday*

(13) Message to Congress (4th December, 1928)

(14) Frederick Lewis Allen, *Only Yesterday*

(15) *Manchester Guardian* (30th October, 1929)

(16) *The Economist* (2nd November, 1929)

(17) *Manchester Guardian* (26th October, 1929)

(18) *Evening Standard* (30th October, 1929)

(19) Frederick Lewis Allen, *Only Yesterday*

(20) *Evening Standard* (30th October, 1929)

(21) *The Economist* (31st May, 1930)

(22) Scott Fitzgerald, *The Great Gatsby*

(23) Derek Patmore, *Private History*

(24) Cornelius Vanderbilt, *Man of the World*

(25) *The Economist* (31st May, 1930)

(26) Robert and Helen Lynd, *Middletown*

(27) *The Economist* (29th October, 1927)

(28) Address to Congress (16th April, 1927)

(29) *Manchester Guardian* (30th October, 1929)

(30) Herbert Hoover, *Memoirs*

(31) John Maynard Keynes, *Unemployment as a World Problem*, Harris Foundation Lectures given at Chicago University (1931)

(32) Address to Pan American Congress reported *The Economist* (14th May, 1927)

(33) Herbert Hoover letter to Andrew Mellon, quoted in Herbert Hoover, *Memoirs* (29th April, 1922)

(34) Oswald Mosley, *My Life*

(35) Herbert Hoover, *Memoirs*

(36) Speech at Poughkeepsie, quoted in Galbraith, *The Great Crash*

(37) Cornelius Vanderbilt, *Man of the World*

(38) Speech in New York (22nd October, 1929), quoted in Galbraith, *The Great Crash*

(39) Frederick Lewis Allen, *Only Yesterday*

(40) *The Economist* (30th November, 1929)

(41) Herbert Hoover, *Memoirs*

(42) *Manchester Guardian* (26th October, 1929)

(43) *The Economist* (2nd November, 1929)

(44) Gerald Heard, *These Hurrying Years* (1934)

(45) *New York Herald Tribune* (24th October, 1929)

(46) *Evening Standard* (30th October, 1929)

(47) Frederick Lewis Allen, *Only Yesterday*

(48) *Manchester Guardian* (25th October, 1929)

(49) *Manchester Guardian* (29th October, 1929)

(50) *New York Herald Tribune* (29th October, 1929)

(51) *New York Herald Tribune* (29th October, 1929)

(52) *The Economist* (2nd November, 1929)

(53) *Ibid*

(54) *Manchester Guardian* (29th October, 1929)

(55) *Evening Standard* (29th October, 1929)

(56) Frederick Lewis Allen, *Only Yesterday*

(57) *New York Times* (10th November, 1929)

(58) *The Economist* (7th December, 1929)

(59) *Manchester Guardian* (26th October, 1929)

(60) Frederick Lewis Allen, *Only Yesterday*

(61) Quoted in Herbert Hoover, *Memoirs*

(62) Address to Congress (1st May, 1930)

(63) Mary Agnes Hamilton, *In America Today*

(64) Herbert Hoover, *Memoirs*

(65) *Ibid*

(66) *Ibid*

(67) *Ibid*

(68) *Ibid*

(69) *Ibid*

(70) John Maynard Keynes, *The Originating Causes of World Unemployment*, Harris Foundation Lectures given at Chicago University (1931)

(71) Lionel Robbins, *The Great Depression* (1934)

(72) John Maynard Keynes, *New Statesman*, article "Gold and the Price Level" (31st January, 1931)

(73) Lionel Robbins, *The Great Depression*

(74) *Hansard* (28th April, 1925)

(75) J. M. Keynes, *New Republic* (20th May, 1925), article "England's Gold Standard"

(76) J. M. Keynes, *New Republic* (16th September, 1925)

(77) *New Republic* (19th June, 1929)

(78) *Ibid*

(79) Speech reported in *Manchester Guardian* (2nd September, 1929)

(80) Hubert Henderson, Memorandum to Committee of Economists (18th September, 1930), reprinted in *The Inter-War*

Years and Other Papers

(81) Hubert Henderson, Treasury memorandum (3rd December, 1943), reprinted in *The Inter-War Years and Other Papers*

(82) J. M. Keynes, *New Republic* (1st May, 1929); article "The Reparation Crisis"

(83) *The Economist* (2nd November, 1929)

(84) *New York Times* (30th August, 1929)

(85) H. V. Hodson, *Slump and Recovery* (1938)

(86) *The Economist* (9th August, 1930)

(87) *New Statesman* (3rd January, 1931)

(88) J. M. Keynes, *New Statesman* (31st January, 1931); article "Gold and the Price Level"

(89) Walton Newbold letter to J. R. MacDonald (1st July, 1930); MacDonald Papers

(90) *The Economist* (21st July, 1930)

(91) *New Statesman* (13th June, 1931)

(92) *Hansard* (19th May, 1930)

(93) *The Economist* (13th April, 1929)

(94) *New York Times* (30th August, 1930)

(95) J. M. Keynes, *New Statesman* (31st January, 1931); article "Gold and the Price Level"

(96) Report of Maclean, International Chamber of Commerce (14th December, 1930); F.O. Papers

(97) Broadcast (29th March, 1931)

(98) Herbert Hoover, *Memoirs*

(99) *The Economist* (30th May, 1931)

(100) Herbert Hoover, *Memoirs*

(101) *New Statesman* (27th June, 1931)

(102) *Ibid*

(103) *Who Can Conquer Unemployment?* (1929)

(104) *Labour's Answer to Lloyd George* (1929)

(105) *Who Can Conquer Unemployment?* (1929)

(106) J. M. Keynes, *New Statesman* (4th February, 1933); article "A Programme for Unemployment"

(107) J. M. Keynes, *New Statesman* (4th June, 1934)

(108) *The Times* (6th May, 1929); report on election pamphlet "Message to Britain"

(109) *Labour's Answer to Lloyd George* (1929)

(110) Hubert Henderson, Economic Advisory Council Memorandum (April, 1930)

(111) *The Economist* (28th September, 1929)

(112) *Manchester Guardian* (25th October, 1929)

(113) Hubert Henderson, Economic Advisory Council Memorandum (April, 1930)

(114) *The Times* (7th June, 1929)

(115) Hubert Henderson, Economic Advisory Council Memorandum (July, 1930); article "The Present Unemployment"

(116) Cabinet Memorandum (23rd October, 1929)

(117) *Hansard* (19th May, 1930)

(118) Cabinet Minute (25th September, 1930)

(119) *Hansard* (28th May, 1930)

(120) Cabinet meeting (19th May, 1930), reported in Thomas Jones, *Whitehall Diary*, edited by Keith Middlemas (1969)

(121) *The Times* (29th May, 1930)

(122) Cabinet Memorandum (23rd

October, 1929)

(123) Oswald Mosley, *My Life*

(124) *The Times* (29th December, 1929)

(125) *The Economist* (24th May, 1930)

(126) Harold Nicolson, *Diary* (30th November, 1930)

(127) *Hansard* (19th May, 1930)

(128) Cabinet Meeting (19th May, 1930), reported in Thomas Jones, *Whitehall Diary*

(129) Labour Party Conference Minutes (7th October, 1930)

(130) Cabinet Meeting (13th May, 1930), reported in Thomas Jones, *Whitehall Diary*

(131) *Hansard* (24th May, 1930)

(132) Cabinet Meeting (14th June, 1930), reported in Thomas Jones, *Whitehall Diary*

(133) *Hansard* (16th December, 1930)

(134) Cabinet Minute (25th September, 1930)

(135) Broadcast reported in *The Times* (29th May, 1929)

(136) Sir C. P. Trevelyan letter to Ramsay MacDonald (21st September, 1930); MacDonald papers

(137) Cabinet Minute (16th December, 1930)

(138) *Hansard* (16th December, 1930)

(139) G. D. H. Cole, *New Statesman* (23rd May, 1931); article "Why We Should Not Reduce Wages"

(140) *Hansard* (12th February, 1931)

(141) *The Times* (12th August, 1931)

(142) *Hansard* (8th September, 1931)

(143) J. M. Keynes, *New Statesman* (15th August, 1931)

(144) *Hansard* (8th September, 1931)

(145) Greenwood's Memorandum on Cabinet proceedings

(146) *The Times* (24th August, 1931)

(147) *Hansard* (21st September, 1931)

(148) *Evening Standard* (26th August, 1931)

(149) Walter Lipmann, *New York Herald Tribune* (10th September, 1931)

(150) Kilmarnock speech (26th September, 1933)

(151) Arthur Greenwood, speech at Colne (6th September, 1931), reported *The Times* (7th September, 1931)

(152) Beatrice Webb's Open Letter to Women's section of Seaham Labour Party

(153) *Hansard* (21st September, 1931)

(154) "Temps" quoted in *New Statesman*, London Diary (26th September, 1931)

(155) Remark attributed to Lord Passfield, formerly Sidney Webb

(156) Broadcast (17th October, 1931)

(157) Speech reported *News Chronicle* (3rd December, 1931)

(158) Ramsay MacDonald letter to Philip Snowden (29th July, 1932); MacDonald papers

(159) *The Times* (5th February, 1932)

(160) *Spectator* (9th December, 1932)

(161) *Hansard* (19th April, 1932)

(162) *Hansard* (13th March, 1933)

(163) *Hansard* (22nd November, 1932)

(164) *Hansard* (13th March, 1933)

(165) *Hansard* (14th April, 1932)

(166) George Orwell, *Coming up for Air* (1939)

(167) George Orwell, *The Road to Wigan Pier* (1936)

(168) *Hansard* (25th April, 1933)

(169) *New Statesman*, London Diary (22nd October, 1932)

(170) *The Times* (9th February, 1932)

(171) Cabinet Minute (8th June, 1932)

(172) *The Economist* (10th September, 1932)

(173) George Orwell, *The Road to Wigan Pier*

(174) *Spectator* (22nd October, 1932)

(175) George Orwell, *The Road to Wigan Pier*

(176) J. B. Priestley, *English Journey* (1933)

(177) Ramsay MacDonald letter to Philip Snowden (29th July, 1932): MacDonald papers

(178) Malcolm MacDonald to Ramsay MacDonald (29th February, 1932); MacDonald papers

(179) H. L. Beales & R. S. Lambert, *Memoirs of the Unemployed* (1934)

(180) George Orwell, *The Road to Wigan Pier*

(181) J. B. Priestley, *English Journey*

(182) Walter Greenwood, *Love on the Dole*

(183) J. B. Priestley, *English Journey*

(184) H. V. Morton, *What I Saw in the Slums* (1933); reprinted from *The Daily Herald*

(185) Thomas Jones letter to Eirene Jones [later White] (10th November, 1932); quoted Thomas Jones *Diary with Letters* (1954)

(186) Walter de la Mare, *The Slum Child* (1933)

(187) *Hansard* (14th April, 1932)

(188) J. B. Priestley, *English Journey* (1933)

(189) *Manchester Guardian* (16th June, 1934)

(190) Reprinted in *Collected Poems* (1955)

(191) Ellen Wilkinson, *The Town that was Murdered*

(192) *Ibid*

(193) Robert Graves & Alan Hodge, *The Long Week-End* (1940)

(194) *Hansard* (17th April, 1934)

(195) *Manchester Guardian* (17th July, 1931)

(196) Hubert Henderson, Memorandum to Committee of Economists (18th September, 1930)

(197) *Hansard* (19th May, 1930)

(198) O. G. Villard letter to Ramsay MacDonald (1st March, 1931); MacDonald papers

(199) Christopher Isherwood, *Mr. Norris Changes Trains* (1935)

(200) F. Yeats Brown, *Spectator* (24th September, 1932); article "Berlin"

(201) C. Delisle Burns, *Spectator* (17th September, 1932); article "Will History Repeat Itself?"

(202) *Economist* (18th July, 1931)

(203) Christopher Isherwood, *Mr. Norris Changes Trains*

(204) *Ibid*

(205) *Economist* (23rd August, 1930)

(206) Lionel Robbins, *The Great Depression*

(207) Graham Greene, *England Made Me* (1935)

(208) *Daily Express* (14th March, 1932)

(209) F. Yeats Brown, *Spectator* (24th September, 1932); article "Berlin"

(210) Edgar Mowrer, *Germany Puts the Clock Back* (1933)

(211) Heiden, *Der Fuehrer*, quoted William Shirer, *The Rise and Fall of the Third Reich*

(212) *The Economist* (18th July, 1931)

(213) F. Yeats Brown, *Spectator* (24th September, 1932); article "Berlin"

(214) Christopher Isherwood, *Mr. Norris Changes Trains*

(215) William Shirer, *Berlin Diary*

(3rd August, 1934)

(216) *New Statesman* (6th May, 1933)

(217) *The Economist* (20th May–10th June, 1933)

(218) *New Statesman* (6th May, 1933)

(219) *New Statesman* (9th December, 1933)

(220) Otto Dietrich, *Mitt Hitler in Die Macht*, quoted William Shirer, *The Rise and Fall of the Third Reich*

(221) *New York Herald Tribune* (13th May, 1933)

(222) Cologne speech quoted *The Economist* (19th August, 1933)

(223) *New Statesman* (4th January, 1934)

(224) Hubert Henderson, Treasury Memorandum (3rd December, 1943)

(225) Otto Dietrich, *Mitt Hitler in Die Macht*, quoted James Laver, *Between the Wars*

(226) Oswald Mosley, *My Life*

(227) Mussolini in Chamber of Deputies (3rd January, 1925), quoted Christopher Hibbert, *Mussolini*

(228) *New Statesman* (24th January, 1931)

(229) Memorandum from Nitti to MacDonald (29th January, 1929); MacDonald papers

(230) *Ibid*

(231) *The Economist* (7th December, 1929)

(232) Memorandum from Sir John Graham to Sir John Simon (2nd August, 1932); F.O. papers

(233) *New Statesman* (24th January, 1931)

(234) Memorandum from Sir John Graham to Sir John Simon (2nd August, 1932); F.O. papers

(235) *New Statesman* (24th January, 1931)

(236) Sir Eric Drummond to Sir John Simon (21st April, 1934); F.O. papers

(237) Memorandum from Sir John Graham to Sir John Simon (29th October, 1932); F.O. papers

(238) Memorandum from Commercial Counsellor to D.O.T. (30th August, 1933)

(239) *The Times* (8th May, 1934)

(240) *The Times* (28th May, 1934)

(241) Memorandum from Nitti to MacDonald (29th January, 1929); MacDonald papers

(242) *The Economist* (1st October, 1932)

(243) *Ibid*

(244) *Spectator* (25th November, 1932)

(245) Oswald Mosley, *My Life*

(246) *Manchester Guardian* (8th June, 1934)

(247) Oswald Mosley, *My Life*

(248) *The Economist* (30th May, 1930)

(249) Mary Agnes Hamilton, *In America Today* (1932)

(250) John Dos Passos, *The 42nd Parallel*

(251) Herbert Hoover, *Memoirs*

(252) Andrew Mellon, quoted in Herbert Hoover, *Memoirs*

(253) Frances Perkins, *The Roosevelt I Knew*

(254) Buffalo speech (20th October, 1930)

(255) Signed statement of Rivers and Harbour Bill (4th July, 1930)

(256) Ray Lyman Wilbur, *Memoirs*

(257) Herbert Hoover, *Essays on Depression and Politics*

(258) *The Economist* (3rd May, 1930)

(259) *Spectator* (29th October, 1932)

(260) *The Economist* (30th November, 1929)

(261) *The Economist* (3rd May, 1930)
(262) Herbert Hoover, *Memoirs*
(263) John Dos Passos, *U.S.A.*
(264) Albany speech (6th October, 1932)
(265) *New York World* (15th October, 1930)
(266) Chicago Convention speech (2nd July, 1932)
(267) Inaugural speech (4th March, 1933)
(268) Broadcast (12th March, 1933), reported *New York Herald Tribune* (13th March, 1933)
(269) *Spectator* (11th November, 1932)
(270) *Manchester Guardian* (4th March, 1933)
(271) *Spectator* (29th October, 1932)
(272) Chatham House *Survey of International Affairs 1933* (1934)
(273) *Time* (1938), quoted in *The New Deal*, edited by Morton Keller
(274) Chicago Convention speech (2nd July, 1932)
(275) Quoted in *Documents of American History*, edited by Henry Steele Commager
(276) Raymond Moley, *After Seven Years* (1939)
(277) Lionel Robbins, *The Great Depression*
(278) William Shirer, *Berlin Diary* (16th September, 1935)
(279) Reported *New York Herald Tribune* (13th May, 1933)
(280) *Manchester Guardian* (4th June, 1934)
(281) *New York Herald Tribune* (17th June, 1933)
(282) *Manchester Guardian* (4th June, 1934)
(283) John Dos Passos, *More Views of Washington*

(284) *Manchester Guardian* (4th June, 1934)
(285) Chatham House *Survey of International Affairs, 1933* (1934)
(286) *New York Herald Tribune* (17th June, 1933)
(287) Herbert Hoover, *Memoirs*
(288) Raymond Moley, *After Seven Years*
(289) Georges Boris, *La Revolution Roosevelt* (1934)
(290) Quoted in Documents of American History, edited by Henry Steele Commager
(291) *New Statesman* (27th May, 1933)
(292) *Review of Reviews* (May, 1933)
(293) *New Statesman* (27th May, 1933)
(294) Broadcast (June, 1934)
(295) Raymond Moley, *After Seven Years*
(296) *Spectator* (29th October, 1932)
(297) *New Statesman* (19th August, 1933)
(298) *Atlantic Monthly* (July, 1955)
(299) *New Statesman* (19th August, 1933)
(300) Sir H. Kennard Memorandum to Henderson (21st April, 1931); F.O. papers
(301) *Daily Express* (15th March, 1932)
(302) *The Times* (21st April, 1932)
(303) Clark Kerr Memorandum to Sir John Simon (29th August, 1932); F.O. papers
(304) M. Speaight Memorandum to Foreign Office (24th October, 1934); F.O. papers
(305) *New Statesman*, London Diary (17th October, 1931)
(306) G. D. H. Cole, *The Intelligent Man's Guide Through World*

Chaos (1932)

(307) F. H. Norman to Ramsay MacDonald (22nd May, 1930); MacDonald papers

(308) Herbert Hoover, *Memoirs*

(309) Frances Perkins, *The Roosevelt I Knew*

(310) Ramsay MacDonald to Ethel Wood (1st December, 1934); MacDonald papers

(311) Oswald Mosley, *My Life*

(312) *Hansard* (12th February, 1931)

(313) Thomas Jones to Dr. Abraham Flexner (16th December, 1934) quoted Thomas Jones, *Diary with Letters* (1954)

(314) J. M. Keynes, *The General Theory of Employment Interest and Money* (1936)

(315) Hubert Henderson, Treasury Memorandum (3rd December, 1943)

(316) Lionel Robbins, *The Great Depression*

(317) Hubert Henderson, Memorandum to Cabinet (24th April, 1930)

(318) Debate in Congress, quoted Arthur Schlesinger, *The Age of Roosevelt*

(319) Herbert Hoover, *Memoirs*

(320) *The Times* (9th February, 1932)

(321) Robert Hunter to Ramsay MacDonald (5th June, 1931); MacDonald papers

(322) *Daily Telegraph* (18th March, 1929)

(323) *Hansard* (16th November, 1931)

(324) *New Statesman* (27th June, 1931)

(325) *Ibid*

(326) O. G. Villard to Ramsay MacDonald (1st March, 1931); MacDonald papers

(327) Ramsay MacDonald to Captain Davis, parliamentary candidate (13th July, 1932); MacDonald papers

(328) Hubert Henderson, Memorandum to Committee of Economists (18th September, 1930)

(329) *New York Times*, London Edition, (11th June, 1933)

(330) Speech at World Economic Conference (12th June, 1933)

(331) John Murray to Sir John Simon (24th August, 1933); F.O. papers

(332) Ramsay MacDonald, private diary entry (18th October, 1933)

(333) J. M. Keynes, *Yale Review* (18th June, 1933)

(334) Lionel Robbins, *New Statesman* (14th March, 1931)

(335) William Shirer, *Berlin Diary* (11th January, 1934)

(336) Lionel Robbins, Journal (24th June, 1944), quoted in R. F. Harrod, *The Life of John Maynard Keynes*

(337) White Paper Cmd 6546 on Final Act of United Nations Monetary and Financial Conference at Bretton Woods (1st July to 22nd July, 1944)

(338) J. M. Keynes, *The General Theory of Employment Interest and Money* (1936)

(339) *Hansard* (21st June, 1944)

(340) *Ibid*

The author and publishers wish to express their gratitude to the Rt. Hon. Malcolm MacDonald for kindly allowing them to draw upon the Ramsay MacDonald papers.

Picture Credits

The Publishers wish to thank the following for their kind permission to reproduce the copyright illustrations on the pages mentioned: Keystone, *frontispiece*; U.P.I., 10, 17, 18, 23 (*right*), 94, 98, 100; the Radio Times Hulton Picture Library, 14, 23 (*left*), 30, 32 (*top and bottom*), 34, 35 (*right and left*), 39, 42 (*right and left*), 49, 59, 61, 68, 72, 73, 75, 80, 83, 110; U.S.I.S., 20, 92, 95; the Mansell Collection, 37, 45, 69, 78 (*right and left*), 85, 89 (*right and left*); Topix, jacket, 48; L.E.A., 54, 62; London Express, 56, 57. Other illustrations appearing in this book are the property of the Wayland Picture Library.

Index